Since When Is Fran Drescher Jewish?

Since When Is
Fran Drescher Jewish?

Dubbing Stereotypes in *The Nanny,*
The Simpsons, and *The Sopranos*

CHIARA FRANCESCA FERRARI
FOREWORD BY JOSEPH STRAUBHAAR

University of Texas Press ✦ *Austin*

Requests for permission to reproduce material from this work should be sent to:
    Permissions
    University of Texas Press
    P.O. Box 7819
    Austin, TX 78713-7819
    www.utexas.edu/utpress/about/bpermission.html

♾ The paper used in this book meets the minimum requirements of ANSI/NISO
Z39.48-1992 (R1997) (Permanence of Paper).

Library of Congress Cataloging-in-Publication Data
Ferrari, Chiara, 1975–
    Since when is Fran Drescher Jewish? : dubbing stereotypes in The nanny, The
Simpsons, and The Sopranos / Chiara Francesca Ferrari ; foreword by Joseph
Straubhaar. — 1st ed.
        p.   cm.
    Includes bibliographical references and index.
    ISBN 978-0-292-72315-3 (cloth : alk. paper)
    1. Minorities on television.   2. Stereotypes (Social psychology)
on television.   3. Ethnicity on television.   4. Dubbing of television
programs.   5. Foreign television programs—Social aspects—Italy.   6. Television
programs—Social aspects—United States.   I. Title.
    PN1992.8.M54F47 2011
        302.230945—dc22

                                                                    2010025058

An earlier version of Chapter 4 appeared as "Dubbing *The Simpsons:* Or How
Groundskeeper Willie Lost His Kilt in Sardinia," *Journal of Film and Video* 61
(2009): 19–37. © 2009 Board of Trustees of the University of Illinois. Used with
permission of the University of Illinois Press.

Ai miei genitori, Franco e Cinzia, per avermi dato la libertà di diventare ciò che volevo.

Ad Andrea . . . "che mai da me non fia diviso."

Contents

Foreword

In this book, Chiara Ferrari introduces us to a critical form of cultural mediation that has largely been unnoticed in decades of debate about the flow and impact of U.S. television in the world. Originally, in the 1970s, scholars and policy makers focused on the large, unbalanced outflow of television programs from the USA to the rest of the world. Those programs were often assumed to have a substantial, direct impact, but researchers who looked at that had a hard time substantiating that assumption. Other researchers began to notice that many audiences began to prefer programming from within their own nations or cultures, seemingly lowering the threat posed by imported U.S. programming. Others began to notice that audiences were not only active in making choices but also in making meaning, interpreting U.S. programs in a way that changed their original meaning. Others noted that there was something of a counter-flow by other TV exporters like Japan, Mexico, and Brazil, whose programs competed with those of the United States.

What went unobserved for a long time was a more detailed examination of the process by which U.S. programs were not only imported into other countries but adapted and changed in the process. Here Dr. Ferrari makes a remarkably original contribution to these debates in international communication, global media studies, and cultural studies by showing in a detailed but clear and lucid way just how much the process of translation of U.S. programs into other languages and cultures changed them in ways that alter the terms of all the debates and research mentioned above. She shows just how much the process of both linguistic and cultural translation of a program like *The Nanny* into Italian for viewers there changed the content and meaning of the program.

In its Italian translation, the story of *The Nanny* is changed substantially from being about a Jewish nanny whose cultural background, speech, and behavior clash amusingly with those of her British employer. In the Italian translation that Dr. Ferrari saw as a child, the story was about an Italian American nanny whose behavior was quite familiar to an Italian viewer. Using this example and several others, she opens up a process that changes the terms of the debate about television flow: that maybe the U.S. programs that swept across the globe were changed substantially in translation before they even reached the viewer so that their impact was already quite different than if the viewers had seen the original program in English.

Stuart Hall talks about how TV programs and all cultural texts are both encoded by a creator who has certain ideas—probably even an intended reading that he hopes the viewer will make—and decoded by a viewer or reader who may well make something quite different of the narrative than what the creator intended. This is a theory that is quite influential in many debates about how TV is created and viewed. Dr. Ferrari introduces a considerable complication to such an approach. What if the initial program is in effect recoded in translation before it ever gets to the viewer? They will then be decoding a work that is not only written, but overwritten or rewritten by a translator from within the viewer's own culture who has changed it into a somewhat different cultural text. They really won't be seeing or decoding the same version of *The Nanny* that someone in the United States did.

A number of researchers are beginning to realize that the creation, flow, and reception of television in the world is a very complex process. Dr. Ferrari brilliantly introduces a new level to that complexity. While she writes specifically about Italy, she also introduces a nice level of theorization about how the larger process of cultural translation of television works. Her close examination of how this works in Italy invites others to imagine and research how this same process of cultural translation may work in other countries and cultures. Our understanding of how the large and very significant flow and impact of television between countries will never be the same as we think about this process of cultural translation and mediation that takes place before the viewer ever sees the programming itself.

Joseph Straubhaar

Acknowledgments

This book is the final result of a long series of modifications applied to an original idea I developed in Arizona. It started as a paper assignment, became a master's thesis, turned into a journal article, eventually grew into a doctoral dissertation, and now is finally a published volume. In what follows I would like to thank all the people who have made this evolution not only possible, but also extremely interesting and gratifying.

This book could not have been written without the wholehearted help, commitment, and enthusiasm of my doctoral dissertation adviser, John T. Caldwell. John is the kind of scholar, mentor, and teacher who elevates his students to their intellectual best, and because of this I will always feel privileged and grateful for working with him.

Together with John, I would like to thank the four members of my dissertation committee at UCLA: Sherry B. Ortner, Steven Ricci, Robert Rosen, and Vivian Sobchack. They have provided me with invaluable suggestions not only to help me complete my dissertation, but also to transform it into a bigger and more ambitious project. The intellectual discussions I've had with them have taught me how to constantly challenge my own research and keep it lively and dynamic.

At the University of Arizona I would like to thank Caren Deming, Mary Beth Haralovich, and Barbara Selznick for nurturing my ideas in their early stages, when I needed it most.

I also want to thank my fellow classmates at UCLA and at the University of Arizona who have helped me tremendously in shaping this project: Rachel E. Adams, Kathryn Bergeron, Emily Carman, Young Eun Chae, Ali Hoffman, Dong Huang-Cherney, Jorgiana Jake, Adam Keller, Andrea F. Kulas, Paul Malcolm, Victoria Meng, Sachiko Mizuno, Rebecca Prime, Maria San Filippo, and Qi Wang. You guys have accompanied me on one of the greatest (and toughest) journeys I've ever taken. The moments I have shared with you are some of the fondest memories I have in both my academic career and life in general.

My gratitude goes to the TV executives, dubbing practitioners, writers, and translators who have shared their experience and knowledge with me, helping me to understand the fascinating world of audiovisual translation: Tonino Accolla, Ludovica Bonanome, Massimo Corizza, Eleonora Di Fortunato, Marion Edwards, Claudio G. Fava, Daniela Nobili, Mario Paolinelli, Sergio Patou-Patucchi, Don Payne, and Gregory Snegoff. Unless otherwise specified, the translation of the Italian interviews and sources originally published in Italian is mine.

At the University of Texas Press my warmest thanks go to Jim Burr for his patience, support, and advice in turning my dissertation into a book. In Texas, I would also like to thank Joseph Straubhaar and Sharon Shahaf for their contagious enthusiasm and the great intellectual discussions we have had on global media studies.

At Chico State I want to express my gratitude to my college dean, Phyllis Fernlund, who has granted me funding, time off, and support to complete this project. Also, I have had the privilege to work under the supervision of a wonderful and compassionate department chair, Terry Curtis. Terry, you are an irreplaceable mentor, a true friend, and one of the kindest men I have ever met.

In Italy, I would like to thank my family—Franco, Cinzia, and Matteo—for their constant, unconditional support, and my friends Luca and Claudia for always inquiring about this project with genuine enthusiasm (and for being the best friends ever!).

My final and special thank-you goes . . .

To Daniel Bernardi for believing in me much before I did, and without whom I would not be the scholar I am today.

Since When Is Fran Drescher Jewish?

The nation fills the void left in the uprooting of communities and kin, and turns that loss into the language of metaphor. Metaphor, as the etymology of the word suggests, transfers the meaning of home and belonging across the "middle passage" . . . across those distances, and cultural differences, that span the imagined community of the nation-people . . .

There must also be a tribe of interpreters of such metaphors—the translators of the dissemination of texts and discourses across cultures.

HOMI BHABHA, *NATION AND NARRATION*

Since When Is Fran Drescher Jewish?

As an international media scholar in the United States, I can say with confidence that I was exposed to "American culture" long before actually moving to America. Clearly, and similar to many other immigrants to the United States, my perception of this country was shaped by endless American movies and television shows that were (and still are) flooding foreign media markets, including my native Italy. What I did not realize at the time was the idea that my perception was strongly influenced by the national environment—and certainly by the national media industry—where I was receiving and consuming these products. I did not question why television, in particular, seemed to offer stories of and about the United States that resonated with my own perception of life, culture, and society. I was pleased to realize that American writers would often choose Italian names for their characters, or mention aspects of Italian history and culture in their plots, or represent aspects of life among Italian immigrants in the United States.

Although Italians generally lack a strong sense of nationalism (with the notable exception of the "soccer craze" during each World Cup), watching "American" television in Italy created in me a feeling of national pride, because I genuinely (or perhaps naïvely) believed that American authors were indeed writing about Italians. At the time lacking any critical eye, I cared little if the characters were portrayed in a stereotypical fashion. Somehow, I thought it was a privilege (and certainly a curious coincidence) that among all ethnicities and nationalities in the United States, American writers would opt to represent and recount stories of Italians. One such show was Fran Drescher's *The Nanny*, in which an exotic and eccentric "Italian American" nanny—or so I thought—revolutionized the life of a British widower and Broadway producer.

It would take me a few years and a few thousand miles to realize (in a classroom, not on TV) that the origins of my favorite nanny had nothing to do with Italy. While discussing ethnic representations on American television with my (American) classmates and professor in graduate school, someone mentioned and criticized Drescher's overly stereotypical portrayal of the Jewish American Princess in *The Nanny*. All of a sudden I was lost: "Since when is Fran Drescher Jewish?" I asked.

That was the day I understood how different the "American" television I had watched in Italy was from the "original" television people were watching in the United States. More important, though, that was the day I discovered the complexities embedded in the process of audiovisual translation. All the references to Italian names, culture, and history, in fact, were created and added *in translation* by writers and dubbing practitioners looking for ways to domesticate American television for Italian audiences. In the case of *The Nanny*, for example, the original Jewish American characters—and their highly caricatured traits—were "erased" and turned into Italian American characters that resonated more easily with Italian humor and Italian audiences.

Since When Is Fran Drescher Jewish? examines the range of negotiations undertaken when foreign countries import globally distributed television programs and adapt them for new national audiences, and reframes the dialogue about relations between the global and the local from a new perspective. This study reexamines the widely accepted (but also increasingly criticized) concept of globalization as a primarily homogenizing force, by analyzing the processes and implications of the translation and dubbing of contemporary American television series for Italian audiences. In doing so, this study moves away from the more traditional—and still dominant—point of view of media "flows" from the *exporting* countries in order to analyze the processes of "indigenization" at play in the *importing* countries. In this respect, the research addresses television translation as an industrial and creative narrative practice closely related to issues of national and cultural identity.

Since When Is Fran Drescher Jewish? analyzes, in particular, the formation of national televisual communities through dubbed TV series, and the consequent indigenization processes performed on these texts in their new national context. Specifically, the case studies focus on the changes made to three American TV series—*The Nanny, The Simpsons,* and *The Sopranos*—imported to Italian television, and examine the reasons why these modifications were considered necessary. In this regard, I examine dubbing both as an industrial imperative and as a form of *cultural ventriloquism*. To do this, I consider audiovisual translation as entailing a complex cross-cultural institutional and *creative* process, making translation something fully implicated in the creation of "new" and "indigenized" texts. The concepts of *indigenization, localization,* and *domestication* used in the book refer to those specific industrial and cultural practices aimed at repurposing television texts for new audiences. This study, in fact, focuses on the efforts made by dubbing practitioners in Italy to rewrite—and therefore recreate—television texts in translation, on the basis of accepted stereotypical notions of what is "indigenous," "local," and "domestic." Specifically, what is at play here is a form of *re-localization,* by which (foreign) cultural depictions of ethnic groups are translated, adapted, and modified to fit a new set of (domestic) cultural stereotypes.

This study provides the field with a twofold argument. First, the book explores the idea that TV translation, and dubbing in particular, should be examined not only as *textual* and *cultural* transfers from one language to another, but as *industrial* practices that facilitate the localization of imported programs. Second, by analyzing the recreation of stereotypical representations of identity *in translation,* the book scrutinizes the *original* tendency of American television to reduce every representation of "Otherness" to the level of stereotype. The ideological implications in this kind of transfer lie in the idea that these representations are translatable precisely because they never cease to be clichés; they are merely reconfigured and transferred from one set of American stereotypes to a new set of stereotypes in the importing country.

At this point, it is worth spending a few words to define the characteristics attached to the specific notions of stereotype I consider in this analysis, given that the term "stereotype" offers a wide variety of interpretations and attributes, depending both on the context in which it is used and the field of study that examines it.

Charles Stangor and Mark Schaller describe the *cultural* analysis of stereotyping as an approach that:

> emphasizes that stereotypes are learned, maintained, and potentially changed through the language and communication of a culture. Language transcends the individual and offers a means of storing stereotypic beliefs at a collective, consensual level.[1]

Stangor and Schaller suggest that every cultural discussion concerning stereotypes should be accompanied by an analysis of the way *language* functions both as a vehicle for the transmission of such stereotypes and as a means to make stereotypes collective. In this respect, Anne Maas and Luciano Arcuri discuss in more detail the importance given to language in the analysis of stereotypes and stereotype formation:

> Although stereotypes may take very different—verbal and nonverbal— forms, language is probably the dominant means by which they are defined, communicated, and assessed. Some authors have even proposed an intrinsic link between stereotypes and language such that there are no alinguistic stereotypes.[2]

Further, they argue:

> embedded in the lexicon of any language at any given moment in history are social beliefs about groups that are automatically "absorbed" during language acquisition.[3]

The above definitions, which include both cultural and linguistic aspects of stereotype formation and transmission, help clarify the key factors in the book's analysis of stereotype *translation*. If it is true, in fact, that "language is probably the dominant means by which [stereotypes] are defined, communicated, and assessed," once television texts are transferred from one language to another, the stereotypes portrayed in such texts inevitably undergo a similar process of transfer and translation. Starting from this premise, my study examines the linguistic as well cultural characteristics of stereotyping; and, considering that the realm of such an analysis is television, the discussion must include issues of representation, which add an inevitable ideological twist to the definitions quoted above.

In the specific case of Italy, such stereotypes mirror the strong regionalism of the country and, more problematically, the allegedly irreconcilable division between the northern, more affluent areas and the rural southern provinces. Through dubbing, then, many of the characters in *The Nanny, The Simpsons,* and *The Sopranos* are culturally and linguistically—but also ideologically—remapped within a new Italian geography based on formulaic myths of the nation.

While not restricting my methodology to the traditional parameters of cultural and reception studies, the book acknowledges the fundamental role of active audiences in the process of transnational decoding of media product and examines the cultural transfer of television texts from one national and industrial context (the United States) to another (Italy). This research directly reflects my own cross-cultural viewing experience as an Italian in the United States; and, while not strictly autobiographical, this book is certainly inspired and enriched by the many personal "textual discoveries" made while watching the same programs on Italian and American television. However, even if the present study only examines a specific binational scenario, the analysis takes into consideration different industrial and marketing strategies in diverse environments and therefore aims at making larger claims about audiovisual translations and media flows at an international level.

To accomplish this, the study that follows employs an interdisciplinary methodology that integrates four approaches: theoretical discussions about "domestication" developed in translation studies, close comparative textual analysis of imported programs, interviews and fieldwork with media practitioners, and economic and industrial analysis from media studies. Such an approach allows one to contextualize the specific cultural changes made to television programs within the broader discussion of repurposing and reformatting media content for international distribution. The study also cites evidence for dubbing as a creative process of cross-cultural textual indigenization performed by television executives, writers, and dubbing practitioners, both in the United States and in Italy, between 2004 and 2007. The interviewees consistently agree that for a program to be successful in a new national context, network executives need to take into consideration the new audience they are addressing and market the products accordingly. Thus, accepting as valid the premise that the bottom-line goal of this "targeted translation" is economic *profit,* the book also discusses how media, and in particular television, have learned to manage, exploit, transform, and adapt cultural specificity as a fundamental industrial practice and proven business strategy in the era of global media commerce.

Case Studies: Translating the Nation

Film scholar Antje Ascheid clarifies the concept of translation as *cultural ventriloquism* by comparing subtitling and dubbing, and the respective possibilities they offer in the construction of "new texts":

> Subtitling, as a dominant practice, serves to constantly remind film and television consumers in the target culture of the cultural and economic supremacy of another, confirming their own lack of cultural expression and independent cultural identity. Dubbing, on the other hand, mostly succeeds in effacing the fact of the film text's foreign origin; or, rather, it gives its new audience the chance to disavow what they really know, hence opening an avenue for cultural ventriloquism through voice post-synchronization.[4]

What is most interesting in Ascheid's discussion is the reference to subtitling as a *dominant* practice—an unusual definition for this method of translation given that, traditionally, dubbing has been considered, at least in film translation, the tool for censorship and ideological manipulation. The quote, in fact, introduces an important aspect of dubbing— *inclusion.* If dubbing indeed erases elements of the original version, at the same time it provides new readings for the new audience and does not necessarily or exclusively entail censorship. While embracing and applying Ascheid's idea of dubbing as a tool for "inclusion," this book argues that this "avenue for cultural ventriloquism" is not automatically constructed as a disavowal of what the audience really knows, but on the contrary may well be an embrace of the traditional stereotypes of the nation, which are used to substitute for the stereotypes in the original narrative.

This analysis of dubbing and translation is relevant to the discussion of global and local media, particularly in relation to the linguistic jokes and language itself in "use"—that is, as a *code* that becomes meaningful in a specific social and cultural context.[5] In terms of linguistic and cultural transfer, then, the recreation of the original meaning usually does not simply lie in a literal translation. A good translator, in fact, should not be particularly concerned about giving an exact paraphrase of the original version. He or she should focus instead on the recreation of those linguistic relations, or "jokes," that will ultimately produce certain reactions in the new audience. The final goal should be to provide spectators with an *understanding* and a *reading* of the new version that comes closest to the original one. Most often, and ironically, this achievement presupposes significant changes from the original version and also justifies use of the term *adaptation* over *translation*. In fact, since modifications are necessary and no direct correspondence can ever be assured, it is paramount to clarify, as Ella Shohat and Robert Stam claim, that "no absolute transparency is possible" since "there remains always a core of mutual incommensurability" between an original text and its translated version. Focus, then, should not be placed "on the 'loss' of an original purity . . . but rather on a dynamic process of cultural recoding, a change in the form of linguistic energy rather than a fall from Edenic purity."[6]

As Yuri Lotman contends, translation—in all its forms—is "a primary mechanism of consciousness," because "to express something in another language is a way of understanding it" and, as I contend, a way to domesticate it and make it familiar.[7] This understanding takes place because the original concept/text is transferred to a new cultural, linguistic, and national framework, which resonates better with the new audiences and therefore allows a closer reading of the original foreign text. Such a transfer in television happens on many levels. *Since When Is Fran Drescher Jewish?*, however, focuses on those changes embedded in the translation of ethnic stereotypes from one national setting to another. In this respect, the book poses several questions concerning the specific modifications made to the programs: (1) What kind of changes are made? (2) What are the reasons for and the ultimate goals of such changes? (3) Is the translation effective in recreating the success the series had in the United States? (4) Is the translation problematic in dealing with and reconfirming stereotypes from one national setting to another? (5) What does the translation of ethnic stereotypes into a new context say about the original tendency of American television to often represent "ethnic" *characters* as *caricatures*? (6) What is the involvement of the network distributing the series in Italy in the decisions about translation? (7) Are the original U.S. producers and distributors aware of these changes, and what is their involvement in the adaptation for foreign markets? (8) What is the creative and professional role of translators and dialogue writers in indigenizing texts for new audiences? (9) Is the erasure of certain elements of the text a form of artistic freedom or a form of censorship?

As these questions anticipate, translation is examined in its broader sense, which includes issues of marketing, programming, and reformatting, in addition to its more common function of the transfer of a text from one language to another.

Chapter Descriptions

The book opens with two broad chapters about television and globalization, and about dubbing and translation, respectively, to set the theoretical, historical, and industrial groundwork for the case studies. The three chapters that follow analyze the three specific TV series already mentioned, *The Nanny, The Simpsons,* and *The Sopranos,* providing evidence for the overall argument that television translation challenges cultural homogenization within globally distributed programs.

Chapter 1, "Nation in Translation: The (Im)Possibility of the Local?" explores the negotiations between the local and the global to understand various factors (economic, cultural, and industrial, among others) that play into the practices of media import and export. In particular, the chapter establishes the argument about the "possibility of the local" within globally distributed television programs, and examines the ways in which audiovisual translation is nothing but an additional example of content reformatting. The chapter also provides a brief overview of certain aspects of Italian geography, history, and culture (including Italian television) to contextualize the specific national environment in which the three series are imported and dubbed.

Chapter 2, "Indigenizing Texts: Television Translation as Cultural Ventriloquism," examines the practices of dubbing television texts and discusses issues of authorship, adaptation, and cultural translation, both from a theoretical perspective and from the point of view of practitioners in the field. This chapter fills some of the gaps between the (thus far) separate discussions of localization/globalization and those of television translation—ultimately showing how the process of "indigenizing" global texts into local cultures can be achieved through dubbing, considered as a form of "cultural ventriloquism" able to create an illusionary and invisible translation for the new audience that promotes and helps constitute the "imagined communities" of the nation.[8] The chapter also discusses the historical role of dubbing in Italy, since the practice has been a traditional and fundamental characteristic of the Italian film and television industry since the Fascist regime in the late 1920s and therefore originated on the basis of ideological and political factors. Since I aim to make broader claims about television translations and the import/export of media texts internationally, the chapter also looks at the economic implications of audiovisual translations and argues that Hollywood has traditionally been strongly dependent on the translation of its films and television programs abroad in order to reach foreign markets.

Chapter 3, "Dubbing Yiddish, Hidden Rabbi: *The Nanny* in Translation," analyzes the first case study, the translation and dubbing of *The Nanny* in Italy, considering the changes made to the series and the reasons behind them. Given the drastic modifications to the overall plot and to some of the major characteristics of the series (e.g., Fran Drescher is transformed from a Jewish New Yorker to an Italian American New Yorker), *The Nanny* is a perfect example to illustrate the processes of indigenizing texts. This series, in particular, shows how a popular U.S. TV program can be made "local," culturally specific, and more appealing in the new national context into which it is imported by changing major elements of the show. One of the strategies used to make the ethnic modification from Jewish to Italian American more effective is the employment of a recurrent U.S. stereotype, the "Jewish mother," which ultimately corresponds to the stereotypical idea of the "Italian mother" in the new national context.

Chapter 4, "Dubbing *The Simpsons:* Or How Groundskeeper Willie Lost His Kilt in Sardinia," analyzes the translation of *The Simpsons* in the process of "indigenization" of the text, in particular through the use of dubbed accents and regional expressions to identify and re-territorialize the secondary characters within the Italian context. The multiplicity of characters and types in *The Simpsons,* whose original depiction is strongly based on cultural U.S. stereotypes, favors and facilitates its translation and adaptation in the Italian framework, especially given the marked differences among regions within the Italian borders. By employing precise national and regional characteristics, specifically those linguistic elements immediately recognizable by the Italian audiences, the translation recreates the ironies and the stereotypical portrayals of the original characters, remapping them in a new (but corresponding) context. A television series as successful as *The Simpsons* is imported in a foreign country and made popular in the new context by "indigenizing" the text and localizing its humor through the use of familiar accents that correspond to local stereotypical cultural types.

Chapter 5, "*The Sopranos* in Italy: Or 'Why Should We Care? We Have the Real Mafia Here!'" examines the translation and reception of *The Sopranos* in Italy, and attempts to understand the reasons for the series' initial relegation to a late-night time slot, despite its widespread popularity in the Unites States. Comparing and contrasting *The Sopranos* with *La Piovra,* an Italian-produced TV series about the Mafia in Sicily, this chapter analyzes the dynamics and the problems of importing foreign programs, especially when such programs discuss themes that might be controversial in the new context. The chapter argues that in the case of *The Sopranos,* several elements concerning organized crime have been domesticated and adapted to the stereotypical idea of southern Italy. However, other elements specifically related to the idea of the Mafia were considered too controversial and problematic for the Italian context, and therefore were either made "foreign" or erased in toto through the translation and dubbing of the series. This case study ultimately shows how the localization of an internationally popular series for a specific national audience does not rely exclusively on *domestication*—as is the case with *The Nanny* and *The Simpsons*—but also on foreignization: the erasure of those elements that might be, somehow, *too* domestic (and, perhaps, problematic and offensive).

The final chapter draws some conclusions from the analyses of the three case studies, and uses the evidence discussed to provide a final definition of dubbing as a form of content reformatting in international media flows. The conclusive remarks reexamine the initial hypotheses about television's ultimate goal in the process of "indigenization" of texts, and consider such goals not only from a cultural perspective but also in economic terms. I close the book raising questions about the dynamics of the industrial practices of media import and television translation, arguing that the bottom-line goal of making texts "localized" is based more on profit than on the "noble interest" of preserving cultural and national specificity. To conclude, I argue that it is fundamental to acknowledge how, in this type of linguistic analysis of television across languages, nations, and cultures, the only effective methodological approach is an interdisciplinary study that must take into consideration both media and translation studies. This combination offers the tools to examine the idea of cultural ventriloquism in truly comprehensive ways: on the one hand, considering the industrial and economic aspects of television in the import and export of media texts; and on the other, applying the theoretical foundation of both media and translation studies to the definition of dubbing as a cultural and ideological practice fully implicated in the creation of new texts and new meanings.

CHAPTER ONE

Nation in Translation:
The (Im)Possibility of the Local?

Dubbing has the power to represent and misrepresent, distort, sway, and in general make a tremendous contribution (positive or negative) to America's image abroad.
CANDACE WHITMAN-LINSEN, *THROUGH THE DUBBING GLASS*

Italian TV: The Most American Television in Europe

The history of Italian television is one of a symbiotic relationship between the TV sector and the state or, more accurately, a relationship between media and politics.[1] Founded in 1944, the national public broadcaster, RAI, was given exclusive broadcast rights a year later, but because of the hardship of the postwar era, regular transmission did not begin until January 1954 and was limited to one channel, RAI 1.[2] The monopoly granted to RAI in the 1940s mirrored the same political monopolistic influence that radio experienced under the Fascist regime of the 1920s and 1930s. RAI, in fact, originated as a development of the radio broadcaster URI (1924), which became EIAR in 1927. This monopolistic approach in radio and television marks a general tendency toward governmental control in Italian media communication, a tendency that was particularly characteristic of television from the 1950s to the 1970s, when the Christian Democratic Party made great use of national broadcasting for propaganda.

Within this strict and politically regulated environment, the general deregulation in the European broadcasting system in the mid-1970s brought fresh air to the television industry in Italy through private cable TV and radio.[3] RAI passed from government control to parliamentary control after the creation of the Commissione Parlamentare di Vigilanza (Parliamentary Supervision Commission) in 1975.[4] In addition, as a consequence of the privatization of the Italian television sector, media mogul Silvio Berlusconi entered the communications arena in 1980, creating his chief channel, Canale 5 (followed by the creation of two additional channels, Italia 1 and Rete 4), and in 1993 founding his Mediaset Group.[5] Since the 1980s, the television system in Italy has remained almost unchanged in its organization, with the exception of Berlusconi's increasing influence in the Italian broadcasting and communication system—influence that has translated into a stronger political role. Berlusconi, in fact, was elected prime minister of Italy in 1994, but his mandate only lasted eight months. In 2001, however, Berlusconi was reelected prime minister, and this time he held power until 2006. Finally, Berlusconi was elected again in 2008 and has been Italy's prime minister ever since. Given the duopolistic nature of Italian television (RAI and Mediaset), considering the direct influence of the state (i.e., the prime minister) on the RAI administration, and bearing in mind that Berlusconi owns Mediaset, during the five years of Berlusconi's second administration the Italian media landscape came under a level of political control that was unprecedented, not only in Italy, but in any major Western democracy.[6] This control was estimated to be close to 90 percent of all the information available to the Italian population, creating a situation that was brought to the attention of the EU because it was seen as seriously threatening Italian democracy.[7]

This brief survey of Italian television history demonstrates how strongly the Italian media landscape has always been related to the state and always highly regulated by governmental and parliamentary dictates. In this scenario, then, one might logically assume that any foreign influence should receive a cold welcome. Paradoxically, however, scholars have argued that Italian television has traditionally and particularly been open to American importation, and this influence has merged with the control of the state in a much more significant way than in any other European country. Communication scholar Giovanni Bechelloni clarifies this relation:

> No other European television, notwithstanding the preoccupations and the mandates of politicians and intellectuals, has been as American as Italian television. "American" not so much in relation to the news—al-

ways prisoners of the national political games—but American in regard to TV fiction and entertainment, particularly after the coming of commercial television in the early 1980s.[8]

What Bechelloni contends is not paradoxical or inexplicable after all: the coexistence of the strong control of the state with the American influence on Italian television is justified by issues of *genre*. News broadcast is notoriously considered a "national genre" because information is often based on local events to which audiences can better relate. Television fiction and entertainment, however, needs to appeal to the viewers based on content, colorful storytelling, and high production values; to many, the United States is undeniably the leading producer in this sector. In regard to television fiction, then, David Morley and Kevin Robins have pointed out the "potential denationalization of Italy: as Italy is seen to incur the danger of becoming an area of pure consumption because of the weakness of its production base."[9] What Morley and Robins do not take into consideration in this process of consumption, however, are the possibilities of indigenization that occur on many levels with micromarketed promotional strategies, reformatting, and audiovisual translations. What is more interesting to examine than the number of foreign products imported to Italy, then, are the complex processes of domestication by which some of these programs become more "Italian."

One contemporary example of "domesticated format" is the game show *Affari tuoi* (Your business), imported as a formula from an original idea developed in the Netherlands by renowned television producer Endemol and sold worldwide, including in the United States, where it airs on NBC as *Deal Or No Deal*.[10] The purpose of the show is for the contestants to win a large sum of money by opening the luckiest box. In other international versions of the show, the boxes are labeled with numbers and are usually opened by anonymous, attractive showgirls who simply display the contents of the box without making any particular comment. In Italy, however, each box is labeled with a number and the name of one of the twenty regions of Italy, and those who open the boxes are common people hailing from each corresponding region. Every time a box is chosen, a traditional folkloric song from that region is played in the TV studio and the show's histrionic moderator, Paolo Bonolis, imitates the accent and dialect of that region in a very stereotypical fashion, exchanging amusing conversations with the person who opened the box (and genuinely speaks with that same accent). Michela Ardizzoni explains the significance of this type of indigenization and argues that it exemplifies the balance of global and local forces in contemporary Italian television:

> This emphasis on regionalism as the essence of national identity expands to other global products like *Big Brother* or *Music Farm*. Aside from the formulaic characterization of participants, this process elicits a contradictory conception of unified identity that is paradoxically fragmented and potentially divisive. In Italy, the presumed homogenizing impact of globalization is confronted with the permeating awareness of regional differences that are frequently accentuated rather than de-emphasized. As clearly evidenced by current news channels, media globalization—the multi-faceted monster condemned and revered by innumerable sources—has produced a sense of immediacy and simultaneity by making us part of common worlds. Yet, at the local level it has been met with deeply rooted realities that defy most attempts of standardizing sub-national experiences.[11]

As demonstrated by the indigenization of international formats, in Italy the major challenge against globalization does not come from a fervent *nationalism,* but rather from the strong *regionalism* with which Italians still identify. Regional stereotypes, in fact, are used continuously, as they represent a well-tested strategy for domestication. When it comes to dubbing, translators and dialogue writers employ very similar tactics to portray characters on television, and rely on the cultural stereotypes that can be conveyed through the use of specific accents and regional dialects. With the strong regionalism of Italy, *regional* stereotypes are often used in translation to adapt *ethnic* stereotypes originally present in the American shows. More specifically, the following section introduces the idea of the "South" (referring to southern Italy) as the imagined—and only—arena for the representation of "Otherness" on Italian television.

Imagining, Narrating, and Translating the Nation

One recurrent complaint from Italian directors of dubbing who supervise the recording of new dialogue for imported television programs concerns the lack of "logical sense" found in the translated scripts they have to adapt for the screen. Daniela Nobili, director of dubbing for *The Sopranos* in Italy, describes one such case:

After years spent in this profession, I still find unforgivable mistakes on paper that I need to correct before the actors can record their dialogue. I give you an example. There are two characters on the screen that meet for the first time and one says to the other, "You're from Texas, right? I can tell from your accent." A literal translation clearly does not make sense in Italy because, if we dub the dialogue, the characters are speaking Italian, so how can one recognize an accent from Texas? In this case, we have two options. We can decide that Texas symbolically corresponds to Tuscany, for example, and we use a Tuscan accent and change the reference the character makes about Texas to a reference about Tuscany. Or we bypass the problem completely and erase the accent and its reference: "You're from Texas, right? I can tell from the way you dress, or the way you walk." We have to come up with a solution that makes sense for the viewers in the new context, and a reference to a Texan accent while speaking Italian does not make any sense at all.[12]

The scenario described by Nobili is but one example of the difficulties and practical problems that dubbing practitioners face when translating and adapting foreign programs for new national audiences. As the situation above reveals, in fact, the ultimate meaning of a text can be lost in translation if the linguistic and cultural references of the original dialogue are not properly transferred or adapted to the new context. As a consequence, the recreation of familiar narratives is often based on stereotypical representations of certain cultural and national *identities* shaped by metaphors of imagined nations and their audiences. In this respect, David Forgacs contends that media, indeed, are one of the most significant factors that shape a nation's identity, and vice versa:

The history of nations has a peculiar close relationship with the history of the media. It also suggests that the media do not reflect or articulate the identity of a pre-existing national community, but are one of the means, maybe even the principal one, by which that community and its identity are brought into being and shaped and later (perhaps) eroded.[13]

Broadcasting plays a particularly significant role in this inextricable relation between media and national identity, since television presents several factors that link it to the nation in perhaps stronger ways than any other kind of media. Linguistically, television programs tend to "speak" the language of the nation in which they are broadcast. More than film, in fact, foreign television programs tend to be dubbed as opposed to subtitled; and, as examined in more depth in Chapter 2, hearing one's native language increases involvement in the viewing experience and reaffirms a sense of national identity. Further, at the level of policy and administration, television networks are usually controlled by national media industries, more or less directly managed by the state. The content and modes of narration of television tend to be very national as well; examples include the news, advertisements, and sports events, which usually focus on national issues. In fact, although not exclusively national, news and commercials represent particular "genres" that more often than others tend to cover and promote national events and products; and with sports broadcasting, identification with specific cities or nations in international competitions is emphasized to the extreme.

In this respect, Italian TV critic Aldo Grasso has argued that television has been traditionally and particularly related to three "histories" of the nation: (1) a history of the forms of *production;* (2) a history of the forms of *representation;* and (3) a history of the forms of *consumption.*[14] Production, representation, and consumption, in fact, are the three forms by which television constructs, narrates, and sells the nation to its audience, according to certain established and imagined myths:

> Television is, at the same time, mirror and amphora of a nation; it reflects the nation's characteristics, but it also shapes a whole system of social relations. With its programming, in fact, television not only illustrates its own content, models, and strategies, but it also designs the traits of an immaterial symbolic community: drawing from the big fish tank of national clichés ("topoi," mythologies, rhetorical apparatuses, styles, traditions, characters, events) [television] creates a "characteristic" image of a nation.[15]

The *image* of a nation, which directly corresponds to its *identity,* is a hard concept to define, as it is shaped by many different constituents and multilayered factors that involve—among others—social, cultural, historical, linguistic, geographical, economic, political, and religious elements. But mapping the forces that have influenced the formation of Italian national identity is fundamental to understanding the logics that drive the production of certain cultural narratives of the nation once foreign television programs are imported, adapted, and dubbed for Italian audiences.

In Italy it has been particularly difficult to create and establish a unified sense of national identity; one major reason for this is what Antonio Gramsci defines as the lack of a "national-popular."[16] Referring to romantic literature and history, Gramsci identifies national-popular (in Europe) as a truly indigenous cultural form of expression, able to address the needs and concerns of the subaltern classes. He cites the French Revolution as the most significant inspirational event for such a concept, because it managed to bring intellectuals and subaltern classes together in the name of national ideals of freedom. In Italy, however, a genuine form of national-popular was never developed, for two major reasons. On the one hand, Italian intellectuals were never able to merge with and write about the subaltern class in truly realist terms. On the other hand, even when such discourses were eventually developed, they were always based on European experiences, and did not address the specific indigenous nature of the Italian subaltern class. These conditions have contributed to the absence of a unified idea of "Italian culture," able to create a popular sense of belonging to the nation. Elaborating on Gramsci's ideas, David Forgacs finds in the lack of the national-popular an important consequence for Italian culture in general:

> As a cultural space . . . Italy has not been strong and effectively homogenized by a powerful Italian national culture over the last century. . . . There has been an unusually high openness to non-national cultural goods, such as to throw into doubt the existence of cohesive "national" culture from the consumer's point of view.[17]

In consumerist terms, in fact, if compared to other European countries with "stronger" national identities, Italy has been particularly exposed to and influenced by foreign products, specifically American products. This tendency most clearly manifested itself during the "miracle years" (1958–1963), when the American lifestyle and glamour became the cultural models to imitate. Such openness to foreign products and the lack of a genuine sense of belonging to the nation uncovers a fundamental reason behind the strong identification Italians feel with their regional environment, more so than with the nation as a whole. During Fascism, Mussolini tried and, to some extent, managed to build a stronger sense of national identity based on the mythical idea of a reborn Roman Empire, contrasting with the strong regionalism of the country, and this idea certainly found some consent among Italians. Such an idea of "heroic" national identity, however, was ultimately imposed through a dictatorial regime, and therefore enthusiasm for a possible "ideological unification" faded with the fall of Fascism.

Howard Moss explains the relation between Italian regionalism and the new European influence on Italy as a way to further understand the weakness of Italian national identity:

> What Fascism did not do, and what, despite all the changes that have taken place in Italy over the last fifty years, no government has succeeded in doing, is significantly to break down the strong regional identity most Italians feel. It is often held up as a paradox that, among the economically advanced European nations, the Italians are the most "regional" yet at the same time the most "European."[18]

Such a relation is not as paradoxical as it might sound, since the identification with the regions and the consequent weak attachment to the nation have facilitated Italians' openness and acceptance of Europe as a progressive move to achieve a balance between the global (EU identity) and the local (regional identity). Italian national identity, in fact, has been "threatened" on at least three fronts. First of all, the idea of Italy as a nation has been weakened on a *sub-national* level (regionalism). Second, Italian national identity has been challenged on a *supra-national* level (the EU). And more recently, the idea of a conservative and unified Italian identity has been questioned on an *extra-national* level by foreign immigration. In this respect, Albert Moran provides an insightful, twofold definition of national identity:

> National identity consists of two parts. It is, on the one hand, a disposition of social inclusion and exclusion, a means of defining who are "we" and who are "them." On the other hand it is also a means of categorization and typification.[19]

Television narratives about the "Italian nation" rely heavily on both aspects of identity described by Moran. The country, in fact, is constructed through a discourse of inclusion and exclusion, and on the basis of highly stereotypical categorizations. Such narratives tend to rely on a traditional idea of Italy picturesquely defined by a regional sense of belonging and conventionally portrayed in its incommensurable division between the North and the South—a type of division that seems to be the only arena for "differentiation" or "Otherness." What is more difficult to find in these narratives, however, is a corresponding description of Italy as an increasingly diverse ethnic and cultural environment that can challenge the static vision of a unified nation-state.

As reported by Italian Caritas in its 2008 dossier on immigration, the number of foreigners (both resident and on a visa) oscillates between 3,800,000 and 4,000,000, out of a total population of 59,619,290. This means that Italy's percentage of immigrants is 6.7 percent (with peaks of 14 percent in Milan and 10 percent in Rome), putting the country slightly over the European Union average of 6 percent (measured in 2006).[20] Such an influx of foreigners with diverse cultural, ethnic, racial, linguistic, and religious backgrounds has altered and continually pushed the Italian population toward greater degrees of multiculturalism. But it seems that television has not been able to depict such a diverse environment in all its complexities, neither through national productions nor in the adaptation of foreign programs. Aldo Grasso describes this tendency and denounces the lack of multiethnic representations of Italian identity on television:

> Italian television in the 1990s seems to *play* the theme of identity more as *Demos* (citizenship, "political" identity) than as *Ethnos* (ethnic identity). Therefore, the emergence of the theme of identity does not translate, so far, in corresponding multicultural politics of programming. (emphasis added)[21]

Grasso refers here to national productions, but this "whitewashing" tendency of Italian television networks is no different in imported programs. In terms of translation and dubbing, in particular, this tendency manifests itself in the modification or complete erasure of ethnic differences, which are usually domesticated and reconstructed according to stereotypical and familiar national narratives. Diversity, therefore, is reestablished according to those regional lines that have traditionally nourished literature and the media in Italy. More specifically than certain generic regional differences, however, "Otherness" on Italian television is often translated into a corresponding "Otherness of the South," considered in a different light than the rest of Italy. The stereotypical idea of the South as "Other" continues to represent one profitable and well-tested cultural narrative of and for the Italian nation. John Dickie has described this dynamic in particularly insightful terms and deserves to be quoted at length:

> More than any other area of Italy, the South has been taken to emblematize the problem of state-formation since 1859. Still today, the power of organized crime in areas of the South dramatizes the failure of the

idea of an impartial state to set down roots: remarks such as "here it is as if we were outside Italy" have been commonplace for over a hundred years. What such sentiments tell us is that the South and concepts of the South are profoundly implicated in definitions of the Italian national space. The Italy counterposed to the South . . . is an ideal, imagined country where, one assumes, clientelism and corruption do not appear. "The South" has also flexible boundaries: it can include or exclude Rome, Sicily, and Sardinia, for example. But few geographical notions can have had such persistent stereotypical associations: the South is where Italians, to say nothing of foreign travelers, have often found their favorite hackneyed images of exotic and/or primitive peasant cultures, dangerous and/or mysterious criminal practices. The South has been made into a theater for "the shock of diversity," whether provoking moral indignation in the spectator, or a fascination for the picturesque. From street corner prejudices to journalistic and academic discourse, the very diverse and changing range of problems within the South, such as those related to economic underdevelopment and organized crime, have too often been thought as the problem of the Otherness of the South, seen as an unchanging whole without internal differences.[22]

Dickie's description covers the multifaceted ideas and ideologies associated with southern Italy and explains the two fundamental tendencies of Italian media toward the South: on the one hand, the picturesque and folkloric image of peasant culture; on the other, the controversial reality of organized crime and economic underdevelopment. The adaptation of American television series for Italian television uses both aspects of the South to transfer these texts into the Italian context. In particular, the translation of *The Nanny* and *The Simpsons* employs the idea of a picturesque South to transfer and *domesticate* American ethnic stereotypes within a new national framework of reference. The translation of *The Sopranos,* however, deals with the more controversial and morally problematic idea of southern Italy as the cradle of the Mafia; therefore, it needs to *foreignize* the text to avoid offending nationalistic feelings.

These examples introduce the multilayered aspects involved with translation and exemplify the general tendency to indigenize texts for national audiences, either by domesticating or displacing national narratives. More problematically, however, these examples testify specifically to the accepted practice of transferring stereotypes in translation, and therefore shed light not only on the new national context in which such stereotypes are *exploited,* but also on the original (American) environment in which these stereotypes are *created.*

Layers of Localization: Dubbing as Content Reformatting

Discussing the impact of globalization on the processes of audiovisual translation, *The Nanny*'s director of dubbing, Massimo Corizza, explains how, until about fifteen years ago, Italians were not particularly familiar with American culture. One of the practical consequences of such "ignorance" was the need to *domesticate* various words in the dialogue that would otherwise be incomprehensible to Italian audiences. Corizza cites food as a particularly thorny element to translate, since Italians, back in the 1990s, had not really been exposed to American cuisine, with the notable exception of fast food. Corizza, therefore, remembers how he was forced to translate "pancakes" with "frittelle" in order to give Italian audiences a better sense of what the characters on the screen were eating.[23] In the new millennium the "American invasion" seems to have influenced the speaking habits of Italians, who nowadays know what pancakes are; therefore translators and dialogue writers do not need to find suitable Italian alternatives for breakfast food when adapting programs for Italian television. If this increased exposure and consequent "knowledge" about the United States are undeniably true, and Italians do know American food and cultural products more than what they used to in the 1990s, it is also true that such exposure and knowledge do not automatically and necessarily translate into a corresponding and unproblematic embrace of the "American lifestyle."[24] The anecdote provided by Corizza helps contextualize dubbing and audiovisual translation within the broader discourse of content reformatting. Dubbing, in fact, is but one way to indigenize a televisual text when "global" programs are imported in specific national environments and need to be adapted for new audiences. Further, however, Corizza's comments introduce the controversial debate about cultural (and media) imperialism, since the scenario described exemplifies the changing relations between the consumption of American products and the ostensible American cultural domination that allegedly follows.

In this respect, global media scholar Albert Moran has contextualized audiovisual translations within the discourse of (media) imperialism, contending that every transfer from one text to another always entails a creative and *active* process of the *production of meaning*, and not merely a *passive acceptance* of the original—dominant—text:

> The translation of texts is invariably the production of a text that is *more than* and *other than* the original. . . . In other words, translation always has a creative dimension: far from the situation of the original text al-

ways imposing an everlasting dominance, even in a translated version, textual translation opens up the possibility of generating a range of texts that are original in their own right. (emphasis added)[25]

Translation, then, finds its legitimate place in media studies when considered as a particular case of *reformatting* within the broader discourse of international media flows. Translation, in fact, is only one method that network executives have available to "indigenize" a foreign text for domestic audiences, and to facilitate its reception at home. Communication scholar Milly Buonanno has defined this process as the "paradigm of indigenization," and has argued that every kind of content or stylistic reformatting allows for forms of *narrative appropriation* by the countries importing American products. Buonanno champions indigenization as a form of "domestication" and defines it as the process by which foreign cultural expressions are re-elaborated, appropriated, and finally transformed into new local cultural forms characterized by domestic specificity.[26]

By substituting the original dialogue with a new sound track, it becomes clear how dubbing fits the characteristics of re-elaboration and appropriation that Buonanno attributes to the idea of textual indigenization. The next chapter examines dubbing historically while also considering its economic implications both in Hollywood and in the Italian media industry. What is fundamental here, however, is to contextualize dubbing as a particular case of reformatting in order to set the groundwork for the analysis of specific case studies discussed later in the book. To clarify the function of dubbing in the dynamic relationship between the global and the local, I consider it useful to visualize the multiple and diverse scenarios that are available for a country's television network. I identify six progressive steps of indigenization—which I call *layers of localization*. These layers represent broad categorizations that include many nuances and whose organization is to be considered open to further interpretation. Nonetheless, the purpose of the following chart is to help visualize and map the role of dubbing in international media flows so as to examine where dubbing stands in comparison with other reformatting strategies.

To clarify the layers of localization, it will be useful to apply these categories to a concrete national example of broadcasting. Let us focus, then, on Italian television as the importing country and on American products as the original programs that are globally distributed. Italian network executives looking for content to fill in their schedule of

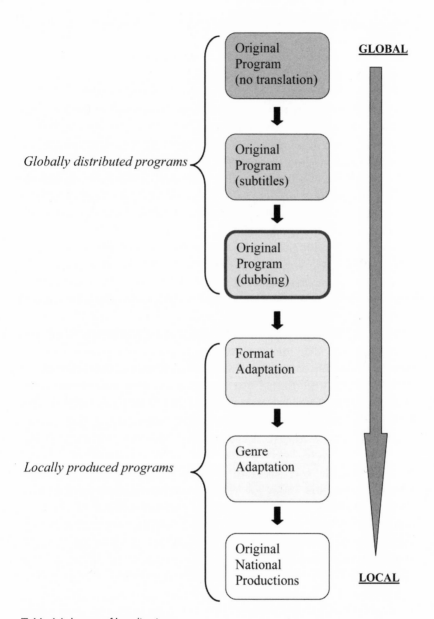

Table 1.1. Layers of Localization

programming will have six different (major) options: (1) they can import a program from the United States (i.e., a TV series) in its original version with no translation, and air it as it aired on the original U.S. network; (2) they can import the same original program, providing Italian subtitles for the Italian audience; (3) they can import again the same program, commission the writing of new dialogue to a dubbing studio, and air the original program dubbed in Italian by voice-over actors; (4) they can buy the format and rights for a successful American program (i.e., a game show or a reality show) and adapt it for the Italian audience, employing Italian actors or contestants; (5) they can appropriate and get inspiration from a specifically "American" genre and modify it according to the Italian taste (i.e., the sitcom or the western); and finally (6) they can produce their own original programming based on Italian stories, Italian sensibilities, "Italian genres" and formats.[27] The combination and intertwining of these categories generate certain sublevels of indigenization, such as remakes, parodies, or co-productions that are located at different stages in the dynamic framework between the global and the local.

Needless to say, the choice of programs to air depends on the targeted audience, the time slot, the familiarity with certain genres and formats, the habit (or lack thereof) of hearing a foreign language on television, and other factors that influence any TV executive who tries to take into consideration his or her national audience while importing globally successful programs. Further, these six broad scenarios intertwine with other factors such as programming and marketing strategies (based again on what is considered more profitable in the new national context), and can offer additional levels of indigenization.[28] Studies on European television show, for example, that the most profitable time slot—prime time—is traditionally and predominantly a slot for nationally produced programs (with the notable exception of American movies, rather than American television series).[29]

In relation to media globalization, academic scholarship has felt the need to address the implications of this dialogue between the "local" and the "global," between the "foreign and imperialist" and the "native," considering all the complexities and nuances of such a "conversation." In particular, Ronald Robertson applies the concept of *glocalization*, adopted in Japanese business for *global localization*, to the realm of international media and communication to explain the diversification of marketing strategies in the exportation of global goods to local markets:

The idea of *glocalization* in its business sense is closely related to what in some contexts is called, in more straightforwardly economic terms, *micromarketing:* the tailoring and advertising of goods and services on a global or near-global basis to increasingly differentiated local and particular markets.[30]

Robertson claims that the exportation of goods from a global environment to specific local realities is not an automatic process that allows for a direct flow from the exporting countries to those who import. If the idea of glocalization is true in economic terms, it is even truer in the media, where exported media forms are not only material goods, but are also cultural products that need to be received and decoded by diverse audiences. This diversity in the reception process depends on many factors, such as language, social and cultural environment, political and economic conditions, and religious beliefs. Therefore, modifications are needed in content and style, but also in programming and marketing strategies, in order for a program to be successful in the new local environment to which it is sold.

In the context of the many options of reformatting outlined in Table 1.1, dubbing holds a strategic position in the spectrum: importing a foreign text and dubbing it in a language different from the original is the "most local" level a network can reach before having to produce its own programming. With formats, genre adaptations, and, of course, original national productions, the symbolic Italian network considered here would have to actively (and more expensively) produce its own shows, even if such shows might be based on well-tested formulas. With dubbing, however, certain "local possibilities" can be explored at a lower cost, because the indigenization happens exclusively at the level of translation, which is less expensive than any kind of original production. The reason why dubbing is charged with so much cultural significance, then, is precisely because the indigenization does not happen in some reformatted or generically "Xeroxed" copy of a television text, but in the modification of that same imported text. With prepackaged formulas and genres cultural appropriation is perhaps more obvious, because these forms include very contingent elements that radically change from the original (actors, production environment, etc.) when a format is imported and adapted in a new country. The cultural implications set in motion by dubbing are much more nuanced, however, and the case studies discussed below offer primary evidence of the possibilities of local manifestations of identity in translation.

CHAPTER TWO

Indigenizing Texts: Television Translation as Cultural Ventriloquism

Fritti Tailchaser: I am in Italy now, I can watch movies here that I have already seen [in the United States]. I am disgusted; can I sue someone in court?
    Please: you have to stop watching dubbed movies!!!
    You cannot understand what a movie really is . . .
Lu Papa: Fritti, have you ever considered in your stars&stripes head that, if all movies were shown in the original version, 9/10 Italians who would like to watch them, wouldn't understand a word?
ONLINE FORUM

Policy and Politics of Translation

In recent years the European Parliament has repeatedly pointed out the necessity of multicultural discussions in order to balance the homogenizing impulses of globalization. Multiculturalism involves diversity on multiple levels—from language to race, from ethnicity to religion—and in Europe it refers specifically to the efforts made by the EU toward developing a "Pan-European identity" while safeguarding the cultural particularity of single-nation members. One way to ensure such diversity is through the support of national media industries that can develop local programs that express their own cultural specificity. Directives such as Television Without Frontiers promote cultural diversity supporting national audiovisual productions and circulation among European countries.[1] However, the efforts made toward multiculturalism in television and mass communications represent only a few of the symptoms involved in the contemporary negotiations between globalizing forces, on the one hand, and persistent inclinations toward diversity. But the debate over multiculturalism in Europe does not focus exclusively on the efforts made to ensure national specificity within the EU. The debate also includes issues surrounding extra-European immigrants, who bring in additional levels of diversity increasingly addressed and expressed in the media.

One of the most significant ways multiculturalism manifests itself in the EU member states is through linguistic diversity, since Europe has been traditionally divided in terms of language, and with the recent flows of immigration such diversity has multiplied. Discussions about multiculturalism, in fact, have expanded into issues of *multilingualism*, considered as an additional step toward the promotion of pluralism. Assuring linguistic diversity allows the survival of national, regional, and local expressions that ultimately correspond to cultural manifestations of identity. As Matthias König contends:

> Language operates as a system of representation providing a socially shared world-view. By providing such a world-view, language plays a crucial role in the constitution of a group consciousness and the symbolization of collective identity. Hence, it is also by its symbolic function that language contributes to social integration. In so far as it fulfills both a communicative and a symbolic function, language is regarded by many socio-linguists as a component of "ethnicity."[2]

Thus, current reconsiderations of accepted guidelines supporting pluralism in the European media sector have included specific amendments about multilingualism, considered an additional (and necessary) step on the way to full multiculturalism. In this respect, it is useful to acknowledge that there are currently twenty-three official languages spoken within the member states of the European Union: Bulgarian, Czech, Danish, Dutch, English, Estonian, Finnish, French, German, Greek, Hungarian, Irish, Italian, Latvian, Lithuanian, Maltese, Polish, Portuguese, Romanian, Slovak, Slovene, Spanish, and Swedish. The list does *not* include: (1) Catalan-Valencian, Galician, Basque, and Mirandese (not nationwide official languages in Spain or Portugal, but co-official languages in their respective regions); (2) nonofficial languages such as Welsh, Gaelic, and Sardinian, among others; (3) all European dialects; (4) Russian (not an official language of the European Union, but widely spoken in those newer member states that were formerly part of the

Soviet Union); and (5) all the languages spoken by immigrants (either coming from European countries, nonmember states of the Union, or non-European countries).

The European Committee on Culture and Education proposed in 2004 a revision of the phrasing of some of the regulations concerning the European media sector, stressing the importance of linguistic as well as cultural diversity. Thus, the general desired goal is now to "preserve and enhance European *linguistic and* cultural diversity" (of the single nation members of the Union and the minority and regional groups within such nations) through "public support to cinema [and other media] at European, national, regional or local levels"—support that "is essential to overcome the sector's difficulties and allow the European audiovisual industry to meet the challenge of globalization."[3] In other words, the EU has found in multilingualism one of the key means to reestablish the "distinctive" traits of national, regional, and local communities, thus providing an alternative to the homogenizing threat of globalization. The document in question reiterates the economic importance to European national media industries of supporting national productions and facilitating distribution. However, the amendments go beyond purely economic aspects of the matter and include concrete proposals aimed at the cultural and linguistic preservation of national/regional cinemas and broadcasting systems. Specifically, the European Committee proposes several regulations dealing with the question of audiovisual translation (i.e., dubbing and subtitling), "with special regard for European lesser-used languages."[4] The aim is to ensure that minority languages are given the same opportunities of translation available to more widely spoken languages. The same goals are the focus of the latest European Media Programme, the fourth of its kind, started in 2007 and to be completed by 2013. As part of its objectives, the European Commission has appointed two media consulting agencies to carry out a close analysis of audiovisual translation practices and needs in the thirty-one nations participating in the project.[5]

Studies concerning European media such as the ones just mentioned have been specifically requested and strongly supported by national associations of dubbing practitioners, such as the Italian organization AIDAC (Associazione Italiana Dialoghisti Adattatori Cine-televisivi). AIDAC has discussed, in somewhat fatalistic terms, the alarming implications of multilingualism in the future of world media markets:

> If we don't want to give in to a single media empire, it is vital to face
> the problems of globalization under a multilingual light. Otherwise, the

countries with lesser-used languages will see their presence in the world media market progressively threatened and compromised.[6]

To consider dubbing as a practice that respects and preserves national and cultural characteristics might sound counterintuitive. Different from subtitling (where the original sound track is maintained and written titles are provided on the screen as translation), dubbing is defined as that process that "involves replacing all, or at least the majority of source language utterances on the original sound track with speech and dialogue in the target language."[7]

The widely accepted idea, then, is that dubbing "hides" the original text and modifies the intentions of the authors to adapt them for the new audiences, and thus ignores some of the very elements (linguistic, cultural, historical, etc.) that initially linked such a text to its specific culture or nation. However, considered in a different light, dubbing becomes one of the major elements that support national and cultural characteristics (specifically those of the countries doing the dubbing). Translation, in other words, is as much about *erasing* the foreign as it is about *including* the "national and domestic." Translation seen from this perspective also shifts the analysis from a production-centric point of view to a reception-centric point of view, and recontextualizes the study of globalization from the perspective of the (American) producers to that of the international audiences decoding their programs. This new point of view provides significant indicators of how globalization and international media flows cannot exclusively be examined as absolute practices of ideological and economic domination.

The present analysis does not aim to judge or defend the practice of dubbing (or, for that matter, any other less "intrusive" forms in which translation occurs). However, whether through dubbing or subtitling, translation is necessary and inevitable in order to reach different audiences, an aspect that is often overlooked by critics and media scholars alike. Further, as argued in the previous chapter, every process of reception by a foreign audience always entails some level of "translation," and dubbing is but one specific case in this decoding process.

This chapter intends to clarify and fill (many) gaps in the common discussions about audiovisual translation in media studies—discussions that have repeatedly focused on a few main theoretical and aesthetic ideas, but have traditionally left out most of the more concrete economic issues at stake.[8] By historically contextualizing the choice of dubbing over subtitling in Italy (first in cinema and later on television), the chapter looks at dubbing as a form of "cultural ventriloquism" that introduces national characteristics within globally distributed television programs.[9]

Fascist Propaganda and Beyond:
Historical and Industrial Aspects of Italian Dubbing

Let us focus, first, on the historical and cultural analysis of dubbing as a Fascist practice of propaganda, with a specific look at the Italian case. Generally speaking, the necessity for dubbing became evident only with the advent of sound in the late 1920s, when "the talking picture became the prisoner of its own language."[10] Most European countries, moved by nationalistic pride and the influx of English-language films, decided to introduce precise protectionist measures in order both to preserve national production and to ensure translations of the films in their own language. Such decisions were important not only from a cultural point of view, but also from an economic one. The American film industry was destined to be profoundly influenced by European market necessities and expectations. The Hollywood studios created specific policies concerning translation and dubbing, and sometimes hired entire casts of foreign actors, directors, and writers.[11] In fact, Hollywood's response to the linguistic demands coming from Europe were diverse, including the option of shooting multi-language versions (MLV) of the same film (a solution "invented and tried out first in Britain in 1929 when E. A. Dupont directed *Atlantic* in English-, German-, and French-speaking versions").[12] Generally speaking, however, the studios favored two different solutions. The first involved using immigrant actors, directors, and screenwriters who could speak different languages, or "importing" entire different casts for the different versions (the method used by MGM, for example). The second option was to create production facilities in Europe, as did Paramount, and shoot the MLVs directly in different countries.[13] Europe was a market that Hollywood certainly did not want to lose, which is why the move toward MLVs was relatively "easy" to make.[14] Nonetheless, the great costs of both options (compounded by the hard times of the Depression) forced the studios to opt for a third, less expensive, method of translation—dubbing, which had already been adopted, but was not completely reliable due to the limited technology in use. Despite its evident advantages in eliminating the shooting of multiple versions, at the time dubbing created problems in several areas, such as synchronization, quality of sound, and, ultimately, the *credibil-*

ity of the new version. As Ginette Vincendeu writes, "Dubbing upset the feeling of unity, of plenitude, of the character, and thus the spectator position. Moreover, it produced in the contemporary audience a feeling of being duped."[15] Considering the poor quality of the first dubbed versions, as well as the audiences' lack of familiarity with dubbing, it is not surprising that spectators were confused and disappointed by products that ultimately looked, and most of all sounded, "fake."

In this environment, Italy prohibited the importation of films in any language other than Italian, and many other countries followed its example (Spain, France, and Germany, among others).[16] A case study analysis of 1920s Italy gives an understandable and specific reason for such a drastic approach: the coming of motion picture sound coincided with the rise of the Fascist Party, led by Benito Mussolini (officially in power between October 1922 and July 1943). Mussolini introduced a political dictatorship based on the preservation and exaltation of Italian national identity and history. Such a vision included banning the use of all words coming from foreign languages, including those that had previously been accepted in the official and commonly spoken language.[17] Clearly enough, this context presented a further pressure for the strengthening of national identities and characteristics, specifically in relation to language.

Between the late 1920s and the early 1930s, film translation and language in film were also central in discussions among Italian critics, who saw in cinema a tool to finally provide Italians with a proper and unified national language (rather than regional dialects).[18] After Hollywood's experiments with MLVs and the establishment of studio facilities in Europe, dubbing finally became part of the national film industries of individual countries. In Italy, specifically, the film production and distribution company Cines began to dub movies in Rome in 1932, using writers and actors who could speak "correct" Italian.[19] Hollywood MLVs, in fact, had often employed immigrants whose native language was strongly mixed with inflections from various Italian dialects, and did not represent the "official" language of the peninsula. Thus, paradoxically, one could argue that Hollywood's MLVs were more "indigenous" than the corresponding translated Italian versions. The language and accents used by the immigrants were more likely to genuinely reflect the "real" Italian spoken in the streets, rather than the bland, unified, "official" language promoted in Italian politics and mass communications but rarely embraced by the general population.

Dubbing movies in Rome became mandatory with a 1933 legislative decree (later made law in 1934). As a consequence, together with the ideological and cultural standardization imposed by the Fascist regime, cinema underwent a similar process of linguistic homogenization. The language in Italian films and in foreign films dubbed into Italian became "correct," but "bland and asexual."[20] Several critics pointed out, at the time and later on, how the language in film, and specifically the artificial Italian used in dubbing, was taken from the theater, deprived of the dialects, and therefore lacked any distinctive expressive characteristics.[21]

Postwar changes in film style and Italian history and society, however, brought a wave of fresh air into the Italian film industry, left in ruins by the economic crisis immediately following the world conflict. Directors such as Vittorio De Sica, Roberto Rossellini, and Luchino Visconti, among others, created what later became known worldwide as *neorealism*, a filmmaking style characterized by shooting on location, often with nonprofessional actors, using natural lighting, long takes, and deep focus to facilitate and free the movement of the actors.[22] By aiming for the impression of realism, neorealist films were often based on improvisation, and thus unexpected problems were commonplace (especially since shooting was done mostly at real locations and, therefore, was rarely under the complete control of the director). Another innovative trait was the actors' heavy use of various accents and dialects during filming. Such regional linguistic expression, instead of being erased in the inevitable practice of post-synchronized dubbing (necessary because of the on-location shooting), were kept intact to increase the sense of realism.

It is unquestionable that neorealism has influenced both Italian and international cinemas on many stylistic levels. Beyond pure aesthetic elements, however, one of the more practical legacies of neorealism for Italian cinema (in the 1950s and 1960s, and still present to this day) was the custom of post-synchronization, as opposed to direct sound recording. Post-synchronization, in fact, was also used systematically in Italian films featuring professional actors, so that its use was not justified by any particular formal, linguistic, or narrative reasons. The results were films that, generally speaking, lacked the vibrant and spontaneous spirit of neorealism and returned to the use of the impersonal, *non-regional* Italian language.[23]

The improbable unified language used in the media was crystallized by another key event in Italian media history. In 1954, RAI broadcast its first program; almost thirty years after cinema, television became the new vehicle through which to "teach" Italians their official, if rarely used, language. Although Italy was unified as a nation in 1861, it really was not until after World War II that Italians freely began to feel and experience that idea of nation and national community—without imposition from the Fascist regime.

Early television in Italy provided a feeling of national belonging by giving Italians the idea of a shared geography, cultural heritage, and means of expression. Linguistic unification, in fact, became a significant mission of television, since the medium now shared the "educational" role of cinema in spreading the national official language throughout the peninsula. Given the limited schedule of television programming at the time, however, cinema still served as the primary medium to expand the use of proper Italian. Considering the number of imported films from the United States after the war, the linguistic question becomes particularly interesting in that most of the films screened were first translated from English and dubbed into Italian. According to Giovanni Bechelloni:

> Paradoxically, the Italian language that all Italians have learned through cinema and television is most likely the language spoken by American actors, dubbed in a literary Italian and pronounced without any dialectical or regional inflection. It's very probable that this is the language Italians have learned to recognize and use, since it was spoken in a narrative context where feeling and emotions were shared, and not the official and jargon-filled language of the news.[24]

The dubbing of foreign films, in fact, continued the tradition of *bella voce e bell'italiano* (beautiful voice and beautiful Italian)—much as did television—emptied of any regional inflection and very much influenced by the rigorous criteria and limitations of theater acting.

Indeed, in 1968 Geoffrey Nowell-Smith harshly criticized the habit of post-synchronization both in Italian and in foreign movie imports later dubbed into Italian. Reiterating the traditional critique of dubbing as a Fascist practice, he claimed that:

> [in Italy] all foreign films are dubbed rather than subtitled, even those for a "minority" or "art" public. Here again a political factor can be discerned at the origins of the procedure, in this case the demands of the Fascist censorship; and again the tendency is towards cultural leveling, but on a world-wide rather than a national scale.[25]

It is hardly surprising that in the late 1960s a film scholar would attack Italian dubbing with such a passionate vigor. After neorealism, these were the years in which the practice of post-synchronization (including in Italian-spoken films) moved from "use" to "abuse" and brought filmmakers such as Antonioni, Bertolucci, Lattuada, Pasolini, and Pontecorvo, among others, to sign a manifesto denouncing the negative effects of dubbing on Italian cinema:

> The post-synchronization of Italian films, when not required for expressive reasons, and the dubbing and translation of foreign films, are the two equally absurd and unacceptable sides of one and the same problem . . . The abolition of the indiscriminate use of dubbing, whose existence compromises the very possibility of an Italian sound cinema, is a vital aspect of the battle to safeguard linguistic research, to protect effective freedom of expression, and to realize and develop a total cinema.[26]

The controversy and the subsequent manifesto of 1968 originated in a time when post-synchronization became the "only" practice adopted in Italian cinema, a sort of permanent mark of awkward filmmaking style not justified by artistic choices and causing actors to grow progressively "detached from the roles they were playing."[27] Nowell-Smith's critique also includes a discussion about the methodical choice, made by Italian filmmakers and directors of dubbing, to eliminate Italian dialects from the dialogue. The problem, according to him, lies in the fact that:

> most Italian actors do not speak the "Tuscan tongue on Roman lips" that is officially regarded as a suitable means of universal communication. Most of them speak dialect, and it should be noted in passing that many of the Italian dialects are richer and more flexible instruments of communication than is the national language. The dialect problem has several consequences. One is that the language spoken in many Italian films is essentially artificial, because it does not correspond to the way the majority of people talk in most parts of the country.[28]

The "Tuscan tongue on Roman lips" refers to the common habit, in film and television, of having Roman actors and actresses erase their original accent, speaking "Tuscan" Italian, traditionally considered the "purest" linguistic form, from which contemporary *correct* Italian has originated.[29]

In such an environment of linguistic leveling and standardization, however, a reaction finally occurred in the 1970s—paradoxically, caused by a foreign film, Francis Ford Coppola's *The Godfather* (1972). The

Corleones' saga offered Italian distributors an "Oscar-winning" (easily marketable) hit with a stellar cast of Italian Americans. The stereotypical features of the protagonists could be clearly recognized by the Italian audience because they were based on a common heritage of local and regional Italian cultural "types." Breaking away from the habit of dubbing foreign movies into an aseptic (and nonexistent) Italian language, translators insisted in the Italian-dubbed version of the movie (titled *Il padrino*) on the use of Sicilian accent and dialect. This choice paved the way for others to employ regional expressions in the dubbing of foreign movies so as to "highlight ethnic, social, and psychological characteristics of the original characters."[30] However, since most of the characters in *The Godfather* are Italian American mobsters, with the exception of a few characters who are actual Sicilians living in Corleone, the dubbed voice-over dialogue needed to highlight that difference through the use of nuanced accents that, on the one hand, could recreate the Italian American inflections of the original characters, and, on the other, could preserve the "real" Sicilian intact. For this reason, the dubbing of *The Godfather* established certain conventions about the translation of Italian American accents that have not changed since. The common practice now used for dubbing Italian American characters is to employ an artificial accent based on southern Italian inflections, mostly Sicilian and Neapolitan, acted out by professional actors who are most likely not originally from Sicily or Naples. Very much like the common practice of the "Tuscan tongue on Roman lips" to recreate "proper" Italian, this technique entails the erasure of the actors' original accent and the substitution of a constructed southern inflection that informs the audience of the "foreignness" of the characters. In *The Godfather* this dubbing method allowed the translation to mark the difference between Sicilians and Italian Americans, the former speaking with a genuine Sicilian accent, and the latter with a constructed southern Italian accent.[31] The spread of such a convention in Italian media has been so broad that the Italian audience is now accustomed to automatically identifying characters as Italian American gangsters just by hearing this artificial accent.

A more contemporary example of this tendency, in fact, is to be found on television, specifically in the Italian version of *The Sopranos*. This will be further analyzed in Chapter 5, as the Italian American origin of the characters translates "well" into Italian for the same reasons *The Godfather* translated well.[32] Daniela Nobili, director of dubbing for the Italian version of the HBO series, clarifies and contextualizes the debate over the use of regional dialects and accents in contemporary Italian audiovisual translation:

[The use of the dialects] is still a valid, though rare, way to recreate linguistic differences. Sometimes we have to be insistent with our commissioners in order to use dialects. In Italy we still have the *icon* of dubbing, using the "beautiful voice and beautiful Italian," but it doesn't mean anything, it doesn't exist anymore in cinema or in television. Often the distributors oppose the use of the dialects, but with *The Sopranos* we had a valid excuse. They are from Naples, actually more specifically, from Avellino, they even filmed an episode in Italy, in Naples. In this case it was easy. But in general it would be very simple to establish hierarchies and diversities through the use of dialects and accents.[33]

Similarly, Tonino Accolla, director of dubbing for *The Simpsons* (and Homer Simpson's Italian voice), reiterates the importance of accents in dubbing as a way to keep film and television language up to date:

As compared to American accents, the Italian ones are stronger, recalling gestures, cultural stereotypes, and characteristics. While American slang renovates and changes, Italian is a "dead" language, which finds it hard to evolve with the evolution of cultures and generations. However, dialects offer very specific information, and one can play with them in many ways.[34]

As Accolla confirms, and as will be analyzed in detail in Chapter 4, the use of regional dialects has been an invaluable strategy through which to indigenize *The Simpsons* for the Italian audience, re-territorializing the stereotypical representation of the characters within an Italian frame of reference. Similarly, the adaptation of *The Nanny* uses accents and dialects to dub Fran Drescher, both to reproduce her Jewish linguistic peculiarities and to highlight the cultural differences between her and her British employer. Generally speaking, then, contemporary writers and directors of dubbing in Italy are partial to the use of dialects and accents not only as a way to recreate the linguistic nuances and hierarchies of the original versions, but also to keep the language current and lively.

Italian Dubbing Industry: A Contemporary Perspective

Daniela Nobili's comments about resistance to the use of dialects from the translation's commissioners introduce the interesting issue of the different roles and responsibilities of the contemporary Italian dubbing industry. Here, I will focus primarily on the processes of television translation since my case studies are television series, but I will also compare these processes to film translation later on. At present, the figures involved in the dubbing of a television series (in order of their "chronological" involvement) are: the Italian distributors, the production supervisors of each series, the translators, the *dialoghisti* (literally, dialogue writers), the directors of dubbing, the voice-over actors, and the synch assistants. The following table visualizes the dubbing process and clarifies the responsibilities of each professional role listed above.

In the past, the roles of the translator and the dialogue writer used to be very much separated: the writer would adapt a translation previously supplied by an official translator. Now, the two figures tend to overlap, and the dialogue writer is also the one performing the translation. The previous list of figures involved in dubbing introduces two main issues right away, specifically at the level of translation per se. First of all, the many steps in the adaptation of a program (sometimes from its original language to English or French—if the language is lesser known—and later to Italian) clearly allow many "domesticated" terms and ideologies to be added and many foreign themes to be erased. This aspect of dubbing lies at the core of its relation to "cultural ventriloquism," which I will discuss in the final section of this chapter. Second, and perhaps less obvious, the lack of clarity in the diverse roles involved with the audiovisual translation causes much controversy in terms of authorship and copyright. The major complaints come from official translators whose professional role has been progressively eliminated. Their argument, explained by Sergio Patou-Patucchi, vice president of the national association of translators and interpreters AITI (Associazione Italiana Traduttori ed Interpreti), lies in the idea that if the role of the translator is eliminated from dubbing, the quality of the adaptation suffers and the original version's deepest meaning is not maintained. According to the translators' point of view, in fact, dialogue writers tend to focus more on lip synchronization than on being faithful to the meaning of the original. Further, even if translators participate in the overall practice of dubbing, usually their work is not officially recognized in the credits and they are systematically underpaid.[35] The argument from the dubbing practitioners rests on the idea that it is precisely the differentiation of the roles between translators and writers that causes translators to go uncredited (since the final names in the credits are those of the dialogue writer and director of dubbing). Translators often do not take into consideration lip synchronization, and no matter how good dialogue might be on paper, it still needs to be modified to match the visuals on the screen. Thus, according to Eleonora Di Fortunato, translator and legal

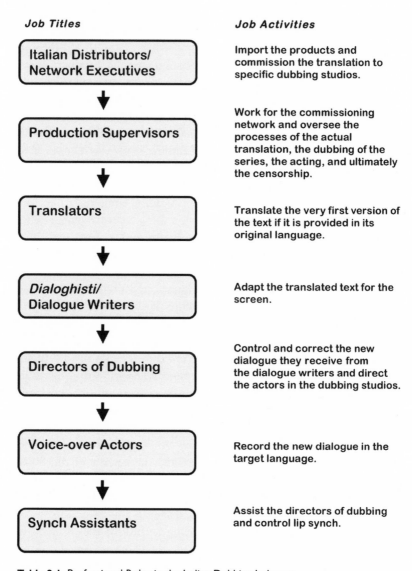

Job Titles

Job Activities

Italian Distributors/ Network Executives

Import the products and commission the translation to specific dubbing studios.

Production Supervisors

Work for the commissioning network and oversee the processes of the actual translation, the dubbing of the series, the acting, and ultimately the censorship.

Translators

Translate the very first version of the text if it is provided in its original language.

***Dialoghisti*/ Dialogue Writers**

Adapt the translated text for the screen.

Directors of Dubbing

Control and correct the new dialogue they receive from the dialogue writers and direct the actors in the dubbing studios.

Voice-over Actors

Record the new dialogue in the target language.

Synch Assistants

Assist the directors of dubbing and control lip synch.

Table 2.1. Professional Roles in the Italian Dubbing Industry

consultant for AIDAC, the two figures should merge in one professional position, which would also give the final work a sense of heightened unity.[36]

These controversies come at a time in which the Italian dubbing industry is finally starting to be seen as significant and therefore mapped within the national film and television industry, although it still struggles to receive official recognition, both professionally and financially. A major step was passage of the regulations of March 2004 (after almost sixty days of strike) safeguarding dialogue writers and their rights over film and television adaptations (the new contract, however, still does not include any regulations about translators, who are considered a separate category). The importance of the document lies in the stipulation of an official contract (to be signed by the commissioner and the dialogue writer) that establishes the specific terms of the job offer, including salary, benefits, subsequent royalties, deadlines for submitting the new dialogue, and so forth.[37] Practically speaking, however, rarely is such a contract signed by both parties, because many nonprofessional dialogue writers accept jobs under the table for lower salaries, causing a drastic and general financial drop in wages for the professional category as a whole. In other words, nonprofessional writers and translators can deliver films and television programs to the distributors and the networks in less time and at a lower cost. Further, the work time networks give to the writers and directors of dubbing to turn in the final dubbed products has progressively decreased. According to dialogue writer and director of dubbing Gregory Snegoff, at present the time limit given to turn in the translation of a feature film is about a week, while optimal working time for a good result would be about three weeks.[38] Needless to say, the overall quality of the final products decreases at the same rate at which time and costs decrease. Although Snegoff discusses the usual time frame allowed in film translation, the situation is not any different in television. This situation derives from very specific industrial factors, not only in Italy but in Europe in general, and is not directly related to the practice of dubbing, but nonetheless strongly influences that aspect of the industry. Indeed, the proliferation of practitioners in the field of dubbing was first caused by the deregulation of the broadcasting system in the early 1980s, when European television saw a significant increase in the number of hours of programming (as discussed in Chapter 1). Channels that used to air only at specific times of the day suddenly needed to fill a twenty-four-hour schedule. Soon national production was unable to fill the demand of the broadcasters; such a shift in the European broadcasting system created the need for more imported programs.[39] Eleonora Di Fortunato and Mario Paolinelli report how, in this environment, 92 percent of fiction on Italian television was imported from various countries, mostly the United States.[40] While Hollywood certainly experienced a significant increase in its international sales after the European media deregulation, such a shift also brought many drastic changes to the dubbing industry. In Italy, in particular, both public and private networks suddenly needed writers and translators to dub the new material:

> The enormous quantity of audiovisual material imported from foreign countries to satisfy (at lower costs) the need of programming for the 900 television networks on the national territory has increased the request for *dialoghisti* (as well as actors specialized in dubbing) and has caused their number to boost from 35–40 (before the advent and deregulation of private television) to about 300, most of whom entered the field in a totally casual way.[41]

This deregulation also provoked a geographical split in the Italian dubbing industry: several dubbing studios were created in Milan, especially for television dubbing, in contrast to the traditional dubbing schools and studios in Rome, usually, but not exclusively, involved with film translation.

A second and more recent deregulatory phase in mass communications has again influenced the industrial practices of dubbing. With the increasing development of cable and digital television in Italy and across Europe during the mid-1990s, broadcasting channels have multiplied, causing a second influx of imported material that needs to be translated and adapted in order to satisfy audience demand. Again, this new deregulation of the media market (not completely stemmed by protectionist directives such as Television Without Frontiers) has further increased competition among dubbing practitioners.[42] Finally, a third factor that has increased the amount of material to be translated and dubbed is the growing market of DVDs that offer several audio tracks in different languages (which also floods the market with new products for post-synchronization even in countries traditionally opting for subtitles).

Controversy is therefore quite common inside the dubbing industry, not only among translators and dialogue writers, but also among the writers themselves and the directors of dubbing. The most frequent arguments concern the quality of the products dubbed and involve polemical statements from members of AIDAC against nonmembers, and vice versa.[43] Overall, dubbing in Italy has received increasing attention in recent years, thanks to the national contract regulations stipulated in 2004. Indeed, after years of dubbing's total absence from theoretical discussions, Italian critics have recently dedicated new attention to the practice, beyond the traditional accusations of linguistic standardization. There is, for example, a new online journal, *ASINC,* devoted to dubbing policy and criticism in Italy launched in October 2005 and publishes both in Italian and English. The major goal of the journal is to provide what is now the only source of criticism about dubbing as a practice and form of creative art. The journal offers updated information about the latest policies on audiovisual translation, in Italy and in Europe, together with interviews with filmmakers, dubbing practitioners, and international distributors.

Also, in 2006 the Italian Film and Television Dubbing Festival "Voci nell'ombra" (Voices in the shadows)—one of the few such in the world—celebrated its tenth anniversary. The festival counts on the presence of renowned film and television critics such as Claudio G. Fava, Morando Morandini, Callisto Cosulich, and others. A significant innovation in the 2005 festival was the launch of a European institution collaborating with the Ministry of Cultural Activities and Assets, created to compare European countries traditionally opting for the practice of dubbing, such as Germany, France, Spain, and Italy; the project aims to inaugurate a European organization monitoring dubbing and multimedia translations that, starting from the Italian experience, can provide practitioners technical and interpretative guidelines while also respecting the original works.[44]

Italy, Hollywood, and Dubbing: An Economic Perspective

Consideration and respect for the original versions of a film or television program have always been at the core of the protests against dubbing by non-Italian filmmakers, who constantly find themselves struggling over their right to present to Italian audiences their original artistic work. This, for example, was the case in the fairly recent attack on dubbing by British filmmaker Clare Peploe, who, while presenting her film *The Triumph of Love* during a press conference at the Venice Film Festival in 2001, strongly voiced her disdain for the practice of post-synchronization in Italy. Once again, her accusations focused mainly on dubbing as the legacy of Fascism. Reactions to Peploe's comments came from both Italian critics and dubbing practitioners, who once again denounced the omission of economics in such discussions.[45] In particular, shortly after the film festival AIDAC published a press release reminding the filmmaker that:

dubbing is not a Fascist inheritance, but a specific commercial strategy of the United States. The practice started with the coming of sound and after a few years of experimentation was exported to Europe. At the end of WWII, part of the funding made available through the Marshall Plan was devoted to film dubbing, and Italy could not resist such practice.[46]

What AIDAC points out here are the economic implications that sound cinema engendered in the film industry—implications that have profoundly altered the relations between the various international audiovisual markets. If there is no doubt that Mussolini in Italy, Hitler in Germany, and Franco in Spain used dubbing for political purposes, it is also true—as AIDAC highlights in the same document—that traditionally democratic France has equally opted for dubbing since the advent of sound. Thus, considering dubbing as only a Fascist imposition means ignoring the fact that the United States has created a global media empire through the translation of their movies and television programs abroad.

The central question, then, is whether it is preferable to consider films or TV programs in their "totality" (thus, also in their potential for distribution, thanks to translation and, specifically, dubbing) or if it is imperative to be rigorous and respect the original intentions of the author, jeopardizing at times the works' potential success abroad. Interestingly enough, the same question is rarely posed for literary translations, considered necessary for the circulation of fictional works beyond national boundaries. The reader might argue that literary translations do not undergo the same process that is characteristic of film and TV distribution. Audiovisual translations must take into consideration lip synch, visual elements in the mise-en-scène, and gestures of the actors. Such concrete limits more often than not are the very causes of the manipulation of the texts, ensuring that they will make sense to the new audiences not only on paper, but also visually.

Surprisingly enough, some answers come from Hollywood and its entertainment industry, which at least publicly and rhetorically has been against the practice of dubbing. In 1992 *Variety* dedicated an article to European dubbing, describing it as an extremely profitable practice for both Europe and the United States. The following is an illuminating quote from the esteemed entertainment publication:

Dubbing has mushroomed into a multimillion-dollar Euro industry. The reason is that many U.S. directors, with an eye to the increasingly offshore markets, are intensely interested in how their films are translated. Another is that a good dub can resurrect a film that performed poorly in the U.S.—dubbing has become more like script doctoring than translating.[47]

Hollywood filmmakers and executives, then, seem to understand the repercussions of dubbing, especially the effect that the translation of their movies and television products has on foreign markets.

In addition, shortly after the controversial 1993 GATT debate over cultural exception from free trade in the market economy, Jack Valenti, then chair of the MPAA, stated: "Do you want to export your movies to America? Dub them!"[48] Valenti was addressing the EU representatives who discussed ways to support European media industries. The proposed strategies included both the imposition of quotas on the importation of U.S. films and TV programs, and the facilitation of European distribution outside Europe through "financial aid in translation, dubbing, printing, subtitling, copying, advertising, [and] establishing relations with other distributors and broadcasters."[49] When asked about her opinion on Valenti's post-GATT comments, Italian filmmaker Liliana Cavani clarified the U.S. position on dubbing:

> Americans have always claimed that watching films in the original version is better: it's easy to say it when you have an [English native-speaking] audience of about half a billion people. Such a refusal by Americans to dub films and the simultaneous flooding of movies to be dubbed in the European market is a true protectionist law.[50]

The economically protectionist aspect described by Liliana Cavani is what is usually left out from the theoretical and aesthetic discussions about dubbing in U.S. media studies. Rarely, if ever, have critics (and filmmakers) who attack dubbing considered the consequences for U.S. media industries of a sudden refusal from European countries to dub U.S. movies and TV programs. As Divina Frau-Meigs clearly puts it, "The impression [is] that the USA refuses to others the advantages they allow themselves."[51] Indeed, Hollywood moguls and television executives have not ignored the economic and financial repercussions of the choice of dubbing over subtitling in most European countries. Beyond Jack Valenti, Fox International Television offers another significant example of the attention dedicated to the European market by U.S. networks. Marion Edwards, executive vice president of international television at Fox, claims that the number one factor in decision making about the production and subsequent launching of a new television show is its *exportability*. Edwards specifies that the potential exportability of a new show influences the choice of one script over another, and that the costs of production come into play only as a secondary factor.[52] In this regard, the idea of exportability described by Edwards finds a direct correspondence with Walter Benjamin's concept of *translatability*. In his famous piece "The Task of the Translator," Benjamin contends that "translation is a mode"; one always needs to start from an original work, understanding the fundamental and intrinsic "law governing the translation: its translatability."[53] By translatability Benjamin means that "specific significance inherent in the original" that lends itself to modification to other languages for other audiences.[54] Expanding on Benjamin's argument, I find such inherent significance to be usually twofold: translatability depends either on the relative universality of the original (a factor that facilitates its transfer to a different culture), or on the possibility of indigenizing the specific elements of the original in relation to the new context. In the context of audiovisual translation, then, *translatability* becomes *exportability* when a program is either globally appealing to diverse audiences, or when it lends itself to processes of localization. Clearly enough, the first case is less risky (and costly) because translation is literal and immediate. The second case, however, requires effort and attention if the most authentic aspects of the original are to be transposed into a different cultural environment. *The Simpsons* is emblematic in this respect. The logic of exportability (and the economic interests that come with it) caused Fox and its coproducer, Gracie Films, to become very involved in the processes of translation for *The Simpsons* abroad. Given the profitability of the series and the merchandising behind it, such interest is not surprising. Fox and Gracie Films sent people to Europe for the first season of *The Simpsons* to audition not only translators but also actors to dub the characters' voices. Although changes have been made over the years, the tendency has always been to try to match the quality of the original voices as much as possible, since they play such a significant role in the humor of the animated show, and in its ultimate success. The Italian production supervisor of the series, Ludovica Bonanome (from Berlusconi's Mediaset), also comments that beyond the attention dedicated to the voices of the characters, much thought has also been given to the translation and adaptation of the jokes and humor, revised in a new Italian light and more comprehensible (and thus more easily marketable) for the new audience. In this respect there is more to say about the peculiar characteristics of dubbing in animated films and TV programs. Dubbing, in fact, is generally accepted with less reluctance in animation than it is in live action. What makes animation more apt for dubbing is, first of all, the fact that even in the original version the characters' voices have to be synchronized with the image; therefore, lip synch is as much of an issue in the original as it is in the translated version. The English dialogue for animation is usually recorded before the visuals are created—a process defined as pre-synchronization. Animators then try to match the movement of the characters' lips according to the prerecorded dialogue available.[55] The final result, however, does not always give the same sense of unity as a real actor speaking with his or her own voice. Once the cartoon is translated and rerecorded, even though the dubbed program cannot be redrawn to match the voice-over actors speaking the new dialogue, there is an established surreal dimension in animation that makes the audience accept certain conventional "ruptures," no matter what language the characters speak. In other words, Homer Simpson's voice is ultimately detached from the actual character on the screen, whether he speaks English or Italian, because in both cases it is an actor in a recording studio who gives Homer his voice. Thus, dubbing is not as intrusive as it is in live-action movies, because it does not break any sense of original unity.

The second reason dubbing is more acceptable in animation is the genre's general impression of lack of verisimilitude and its use of more nonrealistic sound and voice effects than live-action films, a factor that adds to the overall feeling of stylistic exaggeration. Marked (localized) accents, therefore, simply offer an additional humorous element in the already abundant range of extravagant sound effects common in animation. *The Simpsons,* in fact, represents but one case that exemplifies the tendency of using regionalized accents in Italy to increase the comical effect of animated characters. One earlier example of this strategy is the animated saga of *Asterix* (originally produced for television in the late 1960s and later released as various animated and live-action feature films), a French production based on comic books that narrate the adventures of a group of Gauls fighting against Caesar and the Roman Empire. The strategy used by Italian dubbers has been that of dubbing Caesar and all the Roman soldiers with particularly strong contemporary Roman accents and slang. Far from estranging the Italian audience, the indigenization of the characters adds an important comical twist to the general humor of the films, because the stereotypical arrogance usually associated with Romans complements the arrogance of Caesar toward the Gauls. The Italian audience understands the cultural equivalence recreated through the use of a regionalized accent whose use, in this case, is justified by the actual geographic origin of the characters. No one questions the lack of verisimilitude of having Caesar speaking Italian with a Roman accent as opposed to speaking Latin—the actual official language in ancient Rome—because animation allows such atemporal transfers, as long as they work with the overall significance of the story.

The final section of this chapter, then, analyzes these cultural and linguistic correspondences and examines the implications of dubbing as a form of cultural ventriloquism, which on the one hand facilitates the exportation and consumption of audiovisual materials beyond national boundaries, and on the other allows new national elements to be inserted.

Dubbing as Cultural Ventriloquism

Translation scholar Richard Kilborn contends that dubbing represents a tool for the formation of national identities, since:

> the dubbing of foreign language programmes is one way of ensuring that due emphasis is given to the respective national language. *Hearing* your own language spoken not only provides confirmation of its importance and relevance in an increasing homogenized world, it is arguably a more potent way of reinforcing a sense of national identity or autonomy than reading the subtitled text.[56]

Dubbing allows for more possibilities in terms of "manipulation," "nationalization," and "indigenization" of the new texts than does subtitling, and offers an ideal site for a discussion about cultural and national specificity in the industrial (and economic) practices of media import/export. The idea of *cultural ventriloquism,* then, is particularly apt to conceptualize the practices of dubbing as those of "puppeteers" creating "illusions" for their audiences.

Film scholar Antje Ascheid examines the *cultural* implications of *ventriloquism* in film (and television) translation:

> The dubbed film is perceived as an entirely new product. Its leading characters serve not only as ventriloquist's puppets (who are no more expected to produce perfectly matching lip movements than Mickey Mouse); moreover, these *new* characters are uttering a *translated,* which always also means interpreted, appropriated, and recreated new text, thus undergoing fundamental shifts in the construction of their national and cultural identity and context.[57]

Dubbing allows texts to become culturally and nationally specific, not only reconfiguring "myths" for the new audiences in a new context, but also recounting such myths in the very language (including accents, dialects, and regional expressions) of those audiences. Thus, dubbing reinforces, through a heightened illusionary translation process (going beyond lip synch), a sense of national identity and national belonging. Audiovisual translation, and dubbing in particular, make possible and favor the rewriting of exogenous texts as "indigenized" texts. As a consequence, in relation to foreign film or television series, the effective recreation of original linguistic significance usually does not result from a literal translation. Nor is a good translator particularly concerned about merely paraphrasing the original version. He or she focuses instead on the recreation of those linguistic relations that ultimately produce specific feelings and reactions in the audience (with reference to those of the original audience). Most of the time, this achievement presupposes significant changes from the original version more than an exact conversion, and it also justifies the description of the process as *adaptation* rather than "simple" *translation*. As Mario Paolinelli and Eleonora Di Fortunato contend:

> Each culture combines expressive codes according to its own logics. From the diversity of these cultural logics originate the combinatory complexities that make some codes untranslatable. The adaptation deriving from dubbing is nothing but a bridge between different cultures and the writer is its artificer, the author of a tridimensional translation.[58]

Accents as well as dialect and regional idiomatic expressions are elements that profoundly modify the original text. Therefore, dubbing offers a form of "manipulation" depending on several factors that, when combined, may create a significantly different version from the original. Dubbing's potential to change the text thus introduces interesting questions about *authenticity*, as well as about the broader idea of *authorship* in terms of translation and adaptation. Is the new version an entirely new product as well as a new *text*? Such a question aims to understand if, in the end, adaptations offer viewers not only a different program but also a different perception and interpretation of it. According to Antje Ascheid, the dubbed version is an original text, and issues of authenticity are "meaningless" since the "dubbed motion picture becomes a new and fundamentally recontextualized product in the process."[59] Her comment recalls a traditional debate that concerns translators' "frustration" at not being considered "authors." Indeed, national associations of dubbing, such as AIDAC, generally complain about the lack of consideration given to the creative elements introduced by translators in their adaptations. As film and television translator Serafino Murri reminds us, those who rewrite dialogue do not simply translate texts, but "force the linguistic patrimony of a country into a new order of ideas."[60]

In this regard, contemporary translation theorist Lawrence Venuti provides a useful commentary on one of the most influential essays on translation of the nineteenth century, "On the Different Methods of Translation," written by German philosopher Friedrich Schleiermacher in 1813. Venuti explains how, according to Schleiermacher, the translator chooses "between a *domesticating method,* an ethnocentric reduction of the foreign text to target-language cultural values, bringing the author back home, and a *foreignizing method,* an ethnodeviant pressure on those values to register the linguistic cultural difference of the foreign text, sending the reader abroad."[61]

Thus, almost two centuries ago it was already clear that translations modify the text itself in order to establish aesthetic reactions among the new readers. The solution then, straightforwardly explained above, is either to "betray" the author and bring him or her home (i.e., to the *"translating* country") or to "displace" the reader and send him or her abroad (i.e., to the *"translated* country"). In other words, the *bringing home/sending abroad* dynamic is nothing but a double-sided strategy that either modifies the text so that it becomes culturally closer to the new audience (*domestication*), or adapts the original product to highlight those specific elements embedded in the original culture, so that the new audience is confronted with a culturally different environment (*foreignization*). As Italian communication scholar Milly Buonanno contends, *making familiar* an alien phenomenon, or, for that matter, *making strange* a familiar event, represents not only a valid strategy with which to construct *cognitive* patterns for the audience, and thus facilitate the viewers' understanding—it also often allows the development of successful *narrative* approaches that play with specific cultural and national factors appealing to the audience because they are structured around traditional *generic* patterns and national stereotypes and idiosyncrasies.[62] Buonanno defines this process as the "paradigm of indigenization" and argues that every television program, once imported in a new country, inevitably becomes local, and dubbing is only one of the factors involved in this process of indigenization.

The case studies analyzed in the following chapters exemplify the discussion about indigenization, offering concrete examples of the efforts made by Italian networks and dubbers toward both domestication and foreignization. In particular, the Italian version of *The Nanny* offers an example of domestication and imaginative re-territorialization, as the protagonist's ethnicity is modified from Jewish to Italian American. The Italian version of *The Simpsons* offers a similar example of domestication, by adding regional accents through dubbing. In addition, the translation presents elements of actual geographic re-territorialization of some of the characters within Italian borders (specifically Groundskeeper Willie). Finally, the translation of *The Sopranos* presents elements of both domestication and foreignization, since the original program depicts some aspects of Italian American culture—specifically the relation with the Mafia—that are problematic on national Italian television, and therefore need to be recontextualized or even erased.

In this respect, then, language and the practices of dubbing and translation act as tools with which to analyze cultural specificity in the media. Such an approach to translation and dubbing as an active cultural process supports the idea of linguistic formations (vernacular expressions or jokes, for example) as mechanisms able to create and deliver socially significant communication. Specific phrases and idiomatic expressions are related not only to linguistic elements, but also to national and cultural characteristics. The translation of regional expressions and slang, for instance, provides a particularly interesting example of how a translator can adapt uniquely local elements for the new national context in an effective way.

Reestablishing the idea of film and television translation as "ventriloquism," a recent publication on the linguistic and cultural implications of subtitling, *Subtitles: On the Foreignness of Film* (2004), edited by Atom Egoyan and Ian Balfour, further illuminates the general concept of cultural adaptation/translation (even if its focus is not strictly about the practices of dubbing). In particular, Henri Béhar's essay, "Cultural Ventriloquism," echoes and reiterates Ascheid's argument about film translations as cultural practices that represent and voice the local. A practitioner in the field of subtitling, Béhar applies the idea of cultural ventriloquism to the very practices of translation, explaining how, depending on the *effectiveness* of such a translation, the new texts might work with different dynamics in the new context. Béhar claims that:

> subtitling is a form of cultural ventriloquism, and the focus must remain on the puppet, not the puppeteer. Our task as subtitlers is to create subliminal subtitles so in synch with the mood and rhythm of the movie that the audience isn't even aware it is reading. We want not to be noticed.[63]

If applied to dubbing, the idea of cultural ventriloquism works just as well, as the translators' ultimate goal is that of creating an "invisible" new text that is not questioned by the audience (both in terms of the overall meaning and in terms of lip synch). Film translator and director of dubbing Gregory Snegoff claims that the very objective of any film or television translation is to give the impression that the text has not been translated or dubbed at all, thus avoiding the audience's "displacement and disbelief."[64] British television translator Michael Bakewell reinforces this idea in his description of the ultimate purpose of dubbing practitioners:

> The ideal end-product would be the perfect illusion. The best possible response from the audience would be for them never to be aware that we had done anything at all. Dubbing, after all, is the art of being totally inconspicuous.[65]

In Italy, however, dubbing is not always the inconspicuous art that Bakewell describes. The Italian version of *The Nanny*, for example, has been drastically modified through dubbing in the very ethnic and cultural elements on which the original series was based. The shift from New York Jewish humor to Italian American stereotyping often works on the screen for the new audience, since some of the idiosyncrasies are similar. However, Jewish visual elements (Stars of David, synagogues, etc.) appear in several episodes, a fact that causes viewers to experience some mystified detachment from the television experience. Similarly, Groundskeeper Willie in *The Simpsons* is re-territorialized within Italian borders by having him speak with a marked accent from Sardinia, yet he wears a kilt in many episodes—an undeniable visual indication of his original Scottish-ness.

The necessity to justify not only lip synchronization but also the actual visible elements in the mise-en-scène is what makes dubbing a difficult process of cultural adaptation, sometimes successful, other times provoking estrangement in the audience. When dubbing becomes self-referential, introducing historical, social, and national elements deeply rooted in the new context, viewers often have to question its authenticity. Mario Paolinelli, vice president of AIDAC, cites this example:

> Commercial television introduced a new element in television dubbing in the 1980s: self-referentiality, which often becomes self-promotion and self-advertising. In those years, in sit-coms and other television series

one often happens to hear (clearly) American characters refer to places such as *Cologno Monzese* [an area in the hinterland of Milan, hosting the headquarters of Berlusconi's Mediaset] absolutely out of context in the original version.[66]

The Simpsons translator Elena Di Carlo clarifies how the line between domestication and self-referentiality is very thin, describing an exemplary scenario. She explains how, if in *The Simpsons* there is a reference to an American singer who might not be popular in Italy, she needs to find a strategy to modify the text in a way that such a reference becomes clear to the new audience but not detached from the original context. Therefore, the translator can change the referent to Pavarotti, for example, whose name is internationally recognized, but not to an Italian singer only popular in Italy, because that reference would make no logical sense in Springfield.[67] In other words, Bart referring to Pavarotti can represent a good translation strategy for domestication, while a more specifically localized reference only creates distrust in the audience.

The Nanny, The Simpsons, and *The Sopranos* employ all the elements described thus far: the use of accents and dialects; the introduction of specific national, historical, and cultural elements; the transfer of irony; and the use of slang and self-referential allusions. The following chapters analyze each series and the specific factors that allow these American shows—created in the era of *global* television—to become "Italian."

CHAPTER THREE

Dubbing Yiddish, Hidden Rabbi:
The Nanny in Translation

The Nanny is global if it's adapted. In the end, the "Jewish mother" is like the "Italian mother," worried if you don't eat enough, caring for her children, and never minding her own business. The stereotype is very similar, but you have to adapt it.

MASSIMO CORIZZA, DIRECTOR OF DUBBING AND TRANSLATOR
FOR THE ITALIAN VERSION OF *THE NANNY*

The term *burino* is an expression from the Roman dialect that originally referred to people moving to Rome from the rural periphery and the countryside of Lazio (a region in central Italy, whose capital is Rome), either to sell butter, *burro*—from which the term comes— or to look for work in the metropolis. Through time, the burino has come to symbolize people with little education, who are boorish, tacky, and speak a dialect from the countryside periphery. In relation to Fran Drescher's exuberant portrayal of a Jewish American nanny from Queens, New York, in the 1990s hit TV show *The Nanny*, the above description does not seem to have anything to do with the "flashing girl from Flushing." Yet, in the Italian dubbed version of *The Nanny*, Fran Drescher's character is turned into an Italian American whose family originally comes from Frosinone, a relatively small town in the rural area of Lazio known as Ciociaria. Although apparently very different from each other, both the Jewish American and the regional Italian background of the main character stereotypically match Drescher's character's unsophisticated (to say the least) taste, a factor that facilitates the adaptation.

This chapter examines a specific case of television adaptation that highlights the contradictions and problems TV programmers face in their attempt to embrace globalization while trying to appeal to a national audience. The success and the ease of exporting *The Nanny* abroad are not surprising: the general story of a nanny revolutionizing a family routine is nothing new. One only needs to think of *Houseboat* (1958), *Mary Poppins* (1964), or *The Sound of Music* (1965) to identify earlier renowned cinematic examples of eccentric nannies with whom families fall in love. *The Nanny* has been exported worldwide, and reruns are often still on the air in either subtitled or dubbed versions. The show, however, has also been adapted in several countries and sold as a formula. Thus, many are local versions produced in foreign countries with local actors, following a similar plot line to the U.S. version but culturally specific in their dialogue and humor. Such local remakes have been produced in Latin America (Mexico, Ecuador, Chile, Argentina), Poland, Russia, and Greece, to name a few. The Italian case, however, is an interesting example of an adaptation that stands in the middle ground between a more traditional translation and a complete remake. Through dubbing, the Italian version changes significantly in setting and introduces local elements in the dialogue, employing exclusively Italian voice-over actors.

The Italian version of *The Nanny* thus challenges the idea of the global *universality* and *standardization* of imported programs and proposes a new and specific national narrative by modifying the characters and comic elements on which the series was originally based. On the air in the United States on CBS from 1993 to 1999, *The Nanny* tells the story of Fran Fine (Fran Drescher), a young Jewish woman from Flushing, Queens. After being fired by her ex-boyfriend from her job at a bridal shop, Fran arrives at the home of Maxwell Sheffield, a British widower who produces Broadway musicals, to sell cosmetics. Because of fortuitous circumstances, once in Mr. Sheffield's house Fran is hired as the nanny of his three children. A contemporary *Sound of Music* story is then developed. From the pilot episode to the end of the series, in which Fran and Mr. Sheffield finally wed and have twins, the show bases its episodes on humorous gags involving the characters, which also include the nosy British butler, Niles; Maxwell's business associate C. C. Babcock; Fran's mother, Sylvia, and grandmother, Yetta; and Maxwell's three children, Maggie, Brighton, and Gracie. The fundamental comic element of the show is grounded in the clashing and diverse lifestyles of the two families: Fran's eccentric and invasive Jewish relatives and friends juxtaposed with Maxwell's polite and "cold" British lifestyle—or, as Drescher describes it in her autobiography, *Enter Whining,* "blue collar vs. blue blood."[1] In particular, Fran, Sylvia, and Yetta, with their strong accents, "tacky clothes and too much make up," incarnate the stereotypical Jewish/New York woman, which provides a further source of entertainment.[2]

In the Italian version of *The Nanny* (*La tata*) Fran Drescher (named Francesca) loses her Jewish features, and becomes instead an Italian American whose cultural eccentricities and family draw on specific dialectical and regional stereotypes. This is because Francesca's family comes from Ciociaria, situated in the southern area of Lazio. The Italian version, actually, stresses Fran's humble origins by locating part of her family even further south than Ciociaria (on the agricultural periphery of Rome), and has one of her aunts make continuous references to Pozzuoli, a particularly poor town on the outskirts of Naples. As discussed earlier, Italy's most familiar narratives, both in literature and in the media, are often based on issues of North versus South, the former more industrialized and urbanized, the latter more rural. Such a divide is often the major source of both drama and comedy, since not only do the characters portrayed usually reflect the incommensurable separation between the two regions, but they also present comical stereotypical traits highlighted through the conventional use of specific regional accents and expressions. The new humor introduced in the translation of *The Nanny* plays with these conventions and finds a corresponding depiction to the Jewish/New York "whiner"—the uneducated southern Italian—easily recognizable and understandable to Italian spectators. The adaptation thus creates a series that, despite losing its major original comic elements, is successful with its new audience.

In what follows, my analysis will focus on linguistic issues related to the dubbing of the series in Italy and provide an understanding of the reasons behind some of the changes made in the process. What the chapter illustrates is the continued push for national content on television, despite globally distributed (and supposedly homogenous) programs. Through textual analysis of different episodes in both versions, the chapter offers concrete evidence of the cultural aspects that the adaptation takes into consideration in order to appeal to the new Italian audience.

In analyzing *The Nanny*, Barbara Wilinsky talks about both "contradiction within and fascination with" the series, describing it as a "formulaic yet curious television program that both offers another stereotyped vision of Jewish women at the same time it foregrounds and calls into question those stereotypes."[3] Joyce Antler has argued that the two major female stereotypes on which the series is constructed are the *Jewish princess* and the *Jewish mother*, which also happen to be the most derogatory stereotypes that characterize the majority of Jewish women's representation on TV. Fran embodies the Jewish princess—spoiled, whining, materialistic—in all her more conventional characteristics, while the intrusive Jewish mother is effectively portrayed by Renée Taylor, allegedly imitating Drescher's real mother, Sylvia (after whom the character is named).

The Jewish American Princess (JAP) is one of the most recurrent roles for Jewish actresses on U.S. television, and is based on a highly stereotypical view of Jewish American women as self-absorbed, constantly complaining, and snobbish. Fran both embodies and challenges this stereotype. Two of the most evident ways in which Fran embodies her own version of the JAP are her provocative sensuality and her obsession with food, two characteristics not usually included in the highly stereotypical representation of Jewish American women. While these qualities might simply add comic elements to the character's depiction, Fran's (and Sylvia's) overly sexual innuendoes and food obsession also offer a fundamental justification for the change of the nanny from Jewish to Italian American in the translation of the series. Sensuality and love of food, in fact, are familiar stereotypes associated with Italians, both in Italy and abroad; hence these were characteristics that, by being highlighted and recontextualized, could give the new audience comprehensible and plausible reasons for believing Fran as an Italian American. Thus, the idea of the JAP is completely abandoned in the Italian version because it does not match any traditional Italian representation of Jewish women. In Italy, the general stereotypical idea about Jewish people is that they are greedy, a characteristic that Fran does not match. (Although Woody Allen's movies have certainly added a "neurotic twist" to international stereotypes about New York Jews, his representations involve Jewish males almost exclusively, and, at least in Italy, there is no corresponding stereotype for Jewish American women as high-maintenance "princesses"). Fran's comic portrayal of the JAP undeniably offers many gags for the plot, and Fran is still very much depicted as a whining, neurotic single woman even in the Italian adaptation. Nonetheless, although in the U.S. version such traits are conventionally linked to and stereotypically produced by her *ethnic* identity, in the Italian version Fran's whining attitude is detached from any particular ethnic background and is the basis for mere "situational" entertainment.

If the JAP does not match any familiar comic representation for Italian audiences, the intrusive *Jewish mother,* on the other hand, corresponds quite directly to certain stereotypical representations of *Italian mothers.* The "overly caring and concerned" mother, in fact, is a recurrent media stereotype of Italian women and thus more viable than the JAP for the Italian translators. While Sylvia is the "official" intrusive Jewish mother in the series, Fran's position as nanny for Maxwell's children—together with her constant involvement in their activities and personal lives—make her a surrogate Jewish mother as well.[4]

The Italian adaptation, then, modifies most of the stereotypes at the core of the show's humor, recontextualizing them in a corresponding national framework of reference. In particular, the Italian translation focuses on Fran and the women in her family as outgoing, sexually "threatening," and constantly craving food. Sexuality and gluttony are the two elements that are most significantly employed to match the Italian context, because they are, ultimately, already closer to such a context and more familiar for Italian audiences. If these aspects concerning food and sexuality remain unchanged from the original series and are highlighted to justify Fran's Italian American background, other elements, directly related to Fran's ethnicity and religion, needed to be modified to become comprehensible and comic. In losing her Jewish characteristics, then, Fran not only becomes a Catholic—the dominant religion of Italian audiences—but she also loses her ethnic "Otherness."

Dubbing the Jewish Princess and the Jewish Mother: Ethnicity Lost in Translation

Describing the stereotypes associated with Jews in Europe and the United States, Barbara Wilinsky contends, "Many of the qualities which form the Jewish stereotype serve to explain and alleviate the 'threat' of the Jews emerging from their religious differences and supposed economic success."[5] The idea, then, is that in order to be made "innocuous" on and for television, Jews must be portrayed as *caricatures* as opposed to *characters.* Many have thus criticized *The Nanny* and its author, star, and executive producer, Fran Drescher, for her portrayal of a highly caricatured version of a Jewish woman, desperate to get married, moody, and high maintenance. According to *ARTnews* editor Robin Cembalist, the show's "detractors range from Michael Medved, the *New York Post*'s conservative movie critic, to *Lilith,* the Jewish feminist magazine," whose criticism focuses on the lack of interest demonstrated by network executives in portraying Jewish women in a positive light.[6] Yet, "the notoriously nasal nanny . . . is television's most ethnically Jewish character" and offers the only real challenge to the generally bland and assimilated representation of Jewish women on television:

> Many actresses in Ms. Drescher's place would have tried to lose their accent, suppress their big hair and play to Middle America by conforming. Not Ms. Drescher, who is the only reigning Jewish actress on television with the chutzpah to celebrate her ethnic "otherness."[7]

Unlike many female characters on TV whose Jewishness is "invisible" (Monica and Rachel in *Friends* are just one example), Fran's ethnicity is exploited and "exhibited" in a way that perhaps can only be compared to Woody Allen's neurotic cinematic celebration of New York male Jewishness. For Fran, Jewishness is a distinctive mark of her femininity, which could not be expressed in all its complexities without the ethnic element attached to it. According to Joyce Antler, culturally, linguistically, and religiously Fran is characterized as undeniably Jewish:

> Jewishness is, then, an attitude, a phrase, even a set of clothes—glitzy, gaudy, and ornate. It is a shtick, a framing device that sets the heroine apart from the others in the cast. But it is an artificial, exaggerated Jewishness, drawn from anomalous images and negative stereotypes. . . . For the most part, the nanny's Jewishness lies in her inflection, her whine, her Yiddishisms, her mania for shopping and for men, and her Jewish family. Like Fran, they are authentic, whether gaudily overdressed, canasta-playing mother or her chain-smoking Grandma Yetta. But, like Fran, these relatives are without taste and refinement, even without manners . . . it is a vulgar display.[8]

Drescher's vulgar display of Jewishness, therefore, is an example of *performative* identity, an over-the-top expression of ethnic characteristics, based on both "authentic" story lines (inspired by her real family) and on conventional American ideas about Jews on TV. Several scholars (Joyce Antler, Vincent Brook, Barbara Wilinsky, and David Zurawik, among others) have analyzed *The Nanny* at length, examining the controversial balance between Drescher's stereotypical representation of Jewish women and her skill in challenging such a derogative portrayal. The goal of this chapter, then, is to explore this same balance in translation, and analyze the role of dubbing in confirming Drescher's stereotypical traits as an "Italian American," but also its role in favoring regional idiomatic expressions to localize *The Nanny* against the threat of (American) globalization. My focus lies in exploring how such a fundamental aspect of the TV series—the main character's ethnicity—can be modified for a different national context and reconstructed according to the symbolic imagination created by the media in that specific context. What needs to be established by the series's recontextualization, therefore, is a cultural and ethnic background that fits the eccentricity and "vulgar display" of identity on which Drescher originally constructed the show. Further, and as Vincent Brook has interestingly pointed out about the U.S. version, what the translation needs to recreate is Fran's "desire-ability to be both 'other' and 'same,' marginal and mainstream, multicultural and assimilated," which "lies at the heart of *The Nanny*'s fairy-tale premise."[9]

In the Italian version, this balance between "other" and "same" is transferred to the context of southern Italy—a context in which the South is stereotypically constructed and imagined as "Other," and has been traditionally depicted as such in mainstream forms of entertainment. Drescher's cultural and religious "Otherness" is domesticated in the Italian adaptation, by depicting Francesca as an unsophisticated Italian American Catholic whose inappropriate eccentricity and spontaneous behavior clash with her employer's refined but uptight British background. Her ethnic "Otherness" is also domesticated by transferring the Jewish elements to the southern Italian context. For Italian audiences, therefore, Fran is not only culturally familiar as an Italian American or religiously familiar as a Catholic, but she is also ethnically familiar, because her Jewishness is erased. Drescher, therefore, is transformed from Jew to gentile, and this transformation softens the separation between Fran and her boss (and indirectly the audience) because, thanks to dubbing, the difference between the two characters lies exclusively in class and education, not in ethnicity.

There are, however, more profound reasons for Fran Drescher's "move to whiteness." Such a modification to Fran's religion and ethnicity, in fact, is particularly relevant if it is examined in relation to the immigration flow that has characterized Italy in the past twenty years, and that only very recently has been discussed in terms of *integration* as opposed to *assimilation*. Fran's change from Jew to gentile is a sign of that imagined (but fictitious) view of Italian national identity based on "long-lived and anachronistic notions of race and ethnicity."[10] As Michela Ardizzoni contends, such notions consider Italians as ultimately white and displaying "a symptomatic attachment to their language, their religion (Catholicism), their traditions, and their geography."[11] Thus, the main character of a sitcom presenting elements of ethnic, linguistic, and religious diversity to the extent to which Fran does in *The Nanny* does not conform to the standards of Italian-ness perpetrated and sold by Italian television networks.

Such a resistance to use diversity on television, however, is not exclusively Italian. One additional explanation for the ethnic transfer from Jewish American to Italian American in the Italian translation, in fact, might possibly derive from the initial distrust and uneasiness shown by CBS itself at the news that the main character of *The Nanny* would be an "overtly Jewish" woman. Cembalest recounts how Drescher had to fight with CBS executives to "keep her character Jewish"; ironically, they "thought she'd be safer playing Italian."[12] The American network, therefore, thought that marketing diversity would be a winning strategy for its prime-time sitcom, as long as such diversity would be "safe," and thus displayed within the parameters of whiteness.

If even abroad Italian-ness is considered *safer* than Jewish-ness, the Italian translators certainly found a "legitimate" justification for the erasure of any ethnic diversity and the construction of a familiar Italian American originally from southern Italy. Fran's long dark hair and curvy figure allow her to physically pass as Italian, and the family's obsession with food surely completes the transformation. Fran's mother, Sylvia, in particular, offers the ultimate justification for the Italian American theme of the show—even more than Fran—because she is the character that most stereotypically fits the (southern) Italian American type. Massimo Corizza, dialogue writer and director of dubbing for *The Nanny* in Italy, reveals:

> Sylvia is obsessed with food, therefore the Italian stereotype works well, and all the jokes about food remain intact. I had to cut jokes about sex, however, in order to make the dialogue more acceptable; sometimes the original version becomes too vulgar, and too explicit sexual references are hard to transfer on Italian television.[13]

The problems related to the explicit content of Sylvia's (and her mother, Yetta's) sexual innuendoes is solved not only through the use of less risqué jokes, but also through a change in the type of familial relation between Fran and the two women. Sylvia and Yetta, in fact, become Fran's aunts in the translation, since it would be inappropriate on Italian television to have a mother and a grandmother talking so freely and without inhibition about their sex lives. While sexuality on Italian television usually generates less concern than does explicit violence, it is also true that such sexuality needs to meet certain acceptable standards. Given the importance and significance attributed to the family in Italian culture, a mother in her fifties and an octogenarian grandmother openly talking about their sexual lives (including infidelities) certainly does not meet those standards; therefore the series needs to undergo a process of "desexualization." Once again, this example shows how dubbing can manipulate the text in a multiplicity of ways, ranging from cultural references and jokes, to specific linguistic expressions, and, as this case shows, even to the relationships among the characters. All the changes take into account what is considered appropriate and profitable in relation to a symbolic "national" audience that is believed to share certain values, which, in the case of Italy, are strongly shaped by the conservative influence of the Catholic Church.

Massimo Corizza further clarifies the stereotypical correspondence that was employed in the adaptation, and considers such correspondence essential in order to make the show appealing for Italian audiences:

> *The Nanny* is global if it's adapted. In the end, the "Jewish mother" is like the "Italian mother," worried if you don't eat enough, caring for her children, and never minding her own business. The stereotype is very similar, but you have to adapt it.[14]

Corizza's comments testify to the complexity of the idea of a truly global and homogenized culture. The translation of *The Nanny*, in fact, provides a concrete example of *glocalization* and the implicit negotiations at play between the global and the local. The translation of the series indigenizes a stereotype (or in this case, perhaps an archetype—the overly caring mother) that ironically becomes particularized when attached to a specific cultural context. Such a context is the Jewish American setting in the U.S. version and the southern Italian depiction in the Italian adaptation. In other words, the stereotypical portrayal is the same in both versions, but is contextualized and indigenized in the Italian version to become universally understood by diverse audiences.

Throughout the 1990s, drastic modifications to the text such as the ones found in *The Nanny* have been very common on Italian television, particularly in translated and dubbed American sitcoms. Corizza claims that up until very recently many aspects of the United States were not particularly familiar to the Italian public, and therefore translators and dialogue writers had a great deal of freedom in adapting the text to make it comprehensible to the Italian audience.[15] Among the sitcoms of the 1990s *The Nanny* is not an isolated example. Guido Leone, who supervised the dialogue writing and dubbing of *The Nanny* until his death in 1998, was also involved in changes made to a particularly influential sitcom of the 1990s, *Roseanne*. Even in this case the protagonist's cultural background was adapted for Italian audiences, and Roseanne Barr was dubbed with a marked Neapolitan accent. The choice of such an accent to dub a lower-class, outspoken, and unrefined woman provides another example of how southern Italy is seen and constructed on Italian television as an unsophisticated and economically underdeveloped area, and also testifies to the popularity of southern Italian accents on Italian TV and the stereotypical representations attached to them.

Drastic modifications have somehow lessened in more recent years, both because of an increased familiarity with global products seen and accepted as foreign, and also to maintain the overall plot so that it does not lose its consistency and logic in the translation. Nonetheless, significant modifications are still employed in contemporary television programs and often imposed by the Italian networks, perhaps in more subtle ways than this specific case study shows (as will be examined in detail when discussing *The Sopranos*).

Most changes to a dubbed TV show are decided when the first season of a series is first imported and translated, and an acceptable solution is found to be entertaining and therefore profitable for the network distributing the series in the new country. However, problems often arise later when, in subsequent seasons, the plot unexpectedly develops in a direction strongly related to and dependent on the original character's specific cultural and ethnic background. The subsequent adaptations, then, need to resonate both with the original text's development and with the initial changes made in the translated version. Clearly, the more drastic the adaptation is in the beginning, the harder it becomes to find credible solutions later in the series.

The Nanny exemplifies this situation quite well, as the initial and drastic changes to Fran's character proved hard to justify and maintain once the rest of the series was imported by the Italian network Mediaset, and some episodes were strongly based on Jewish elements. The major difficulties were in two main areas. The first was the increasing use of Yiddish words throughout the series. This language undeniably defined Fran as Jewish American, and needed to be linguistically adapted to make sense in the Italian American/southern Italian context. The second was that some episodes featured many "indisputably Jewish" visual elements or characters (Stars of David, menorahs, synagogues, cantors, rabbis), which not only highlighted the Jewishness of the show but also could not materially be erased from the screen. In both cases these difficulties were overcome through the use of dubbing and changes to the dialogue, sometimes more successfully, other times leaving the Italian audience wondering about the credibility of certain choices.

A Nanny from Queens to Ciociaria:
How Fran Drescher Becomes a Burina

Generally speaking, the fact that part of a show's humor is strongly based on specific verbal expressions causes problems in the new version, because translators must either erase the linguistic jokes or try to find acceptable alternatives that can make sense and be funny in the new context. The recognition of adaptations as an active cultural process supports the idea of linguistic manifestations (regional expressions or linguistic jokes, for example) as mechanisms that create and deliver social significance. Linguistic jokes, in fact, often belong more to what could be defined as *popular wisdom* than to "standard" humor. Therefore, in the process of adaptation, translators encounter several difficulties when they try to recreate similar meanings and effects for the new audience. Further, specific phrases and idiomatic expressions are related not only to linguistic elements, but also to national and cultural characteristics, as the use of Yiddish in *The Nanny* demonstrates. The translation of specific linguistic expressions and slang, in fact, provides a particularly interesting example of how a translator can adapt peculiar regional jokes or colloquial expressions to effectively recreate cultural significance. Again, it is important to remember that "effective" in this instance means "understandable."[16]

These factors are essential to the Italian adaptation of *The Nanny*. Although Francesca does not speak with a particular accent (itself a big change from the original, in which Fran's thick New York/Queens accent is quite important), her background is clearly understandable through her use of dialectical expressions from Ciociaria and her less-than-sophisticated attitude, which recalls the rural periphery and the overall stereotype of the burina. In addition, her family name—Cacace—to an Italian audience, immediately sounds southern Italian. Francesca's family name thus informs the audience about important aspects of the character, who seems to be portrayed in a less positive light than Fran in the American version. In the United States, the nanny's family name is Fine. By being called Miss *Fine,* Fran is automatically presented as a likeable—that is, fine—character and to some extent raised to a higher level than the other characters on the show. Cacace, however, is usually perceived in Italy as a tacky and humorous last name, which, beyond establishing Francesca's origin in the South, adds a touch of vulgarity to her representation (the last name Cacace clearly recalls the word *cacca,* commonly used in Italian for excrement). Both the U.S. and the Italian versions, however, introduce the nanny's characteristics very clearly: her eccentricity and self-confidence are evident in the way she looks (strong makeup, tight clothes) but also in her attitude with Maxwell (she writes her resume with lipstick and answers a phone call in the house when the butler is not available).

The "tone" used in the conversation is another interesting element to take into consideration in the analysis of *The Nanny.* Tone, considered in this case for its connotation of style or manner of expression in speaking or writing, usually helps express not only the different moods of the characters but also the nature of their specific interactions. A good example can be found in the pronouns used to address the characters, defined in Italian as *forme allocutive* (*lei* more formal, usually used to show respect especially toward older people, and *tu* more direct and informal, used among friends and people of the same age).[17] In English there is only one form of "you," thus, in the translation from English to Italian this type of linguistic adaptation usually requires translators to take a specific position in respect to the characters. By choosing one or the other form translators establish specific relations and social statuses. *La tata* undergoes this adaptation process by having different characters address one another with different pronouns, depending on the characters' relationships (for example, Francesca and Maxwell both use the formal *lei* mode for each other, Maxwell uses the familiar *tu* form with the butler, Niles, while Niles addresses Maxwell with *lei*). Therefore, in the Italian version the social and economic gap between characters is to some extent more evident than in the U.S. version.

Analysis of language in *The Nanny,* however, yields even more information about the characters and their relationship. In the original U.S. version Fran's linguistic performance is characterized by three other strongly stereotypical traits: her nasal voice, her thick Queens accent, and her use of Yiddish. Probably the most distinctive aspect of the series, Drescher's (real) "fingernails on a chalk board" nasal voice is one more sign of her Jewishness, together with all the other Jewish female characters in the series who tend to speak in a highly nasal pitch. However, while in the United States nasal voices are often stereotypically associated with Jewish people, in Italy the tone of Fran's voice—which is to some extent reproduced by the voice-over actress—is detached from any ethnic element and becomes a more "neutral" factor for comedy. Fran's nasal voice, then, much like her whining attitude, is maintained for the sake of comedy, but is "whitened" and detached from her origin.

A different kind of domestication happens with the use of her accent and her use of Yiddish. The thick New York inflection that characterizes Fran in the U.S. version and separates her from Maxwell's sophisticated British accent is *not* transferred to the Italian context. Contrary to what happened with *Roseanne,* whose original Southern accent was turned into an inflection from Apulia, Fran's original New York accent is erased and not translated to a regional Italian context. Rather, the indigenization happens on a different level, and is translated to the dialect of southern Lazio. In this regard it is important to again remember the difference between speaking Italian with a regional *accent* and speaking in a regional *dialect,* the latter involving not only the use of a different inflection but also the use of words completely different from standard Italian.

In regard to the linguistic gap between Fran and Maxwell, in Italian film and television it is conventionally accepted that the distinction between British and American English is not translated through the use of different Italian accents, but rather through the use of a more sophisticated Italian for characters originally from Britain than the Italian used to dub characters originally from the United States. The difference in this instance, therefore, lies in the choice of vocabulary more than in the choice of accent. Thus, Maxwell is not dubbed with a British Italian accent because this is an old-fashioned strategy popularly associated with parodies of Laurel and Hardy (famously dubbed in Italy with exaggerated British accents by Mauro Zambuto and Alberto Sordi). The convention in *The Nanny,* then, is having her British employer use more sophisticated terms than Fran does; as Corizza recounts, "it works, because not only does Fran speak a less sophisticated Italian, but she also speaks dialect, an aspect that makes her particularly stand out within Maxwell's family, like Yiddish does in the original version."[18]

Writing about the U.S. version, Wilinsky analyzes the linguistic separation among characters both culturally and ethnically, and argues that the gap between Fran and Maxwell is based more on class than ethnicity:

Fran's coding as working class is further associated with her language. Mr. Sheffield often uses words, frequently French, that Fran does not understand. . . . As Drescher expected, this confusion of language based on class disperses some of the tension surrounding Fran's ethnicity by emphasizing and finding comedy in her lack of "culture" rather than her Jewishness.[19]

What Wilinsky focuses on here is the linguistic divide based on social status and dictated by Maxwell's sophisticated use of English or French, which Fran cannot understand because of her lack of education. What is more interesting to me, however, is the ethnic and linguistic divide produced by Fran's use of Yiddish. In this case, "the tension surrounding Fran's ethnicity" is not dispersed but rather emphasized. Thus, linguistically Fran's character is most strongly and affirmatively defined by her own ethnic identity than by her unsophisticated cultural background. In other words, if compared to Maxwell, Fran is characterized more significantly by what she "ethnically" *is* than by what "socially" she *is not*. Therefore, language in particular legitimizes Fran as Jewish. Further, the use of "incomprehensible" words is a strong comic element in *The Nanny*, since both Fran and Sylvia often use Yiddish to communicate among themselves as a type of exclusive linguistic code. As Wilinsky writes:

> One of the main characteristics attributed to Jews is a unique relationship to language. To the non-Jew, European Jews seem to possess a "hidden" language—Yiddish—that others cannot understand and that may be used in subversive ways.[20]

The use of a "subversive" language is one of the most significant aspects that characterize Fran as Jewish in the U.S. version. The use of Yiddish in the U.S. version justifies the dubbed use of words from the dialect in the Italian version as a way to reproduce that "hidden" original language that so clearly identifies Fran. In fact, all the idioms from Ciociaria employed in the translation "cover" and correspond to Fran's use of Yiddish as a way to stand out among the rest of the gentile characters. However, the new context in which she stands out is not a world of Jews and gentiles, but the world of tacky southern Italians and a sophisticated British family.

A particularly interesting aspect in the analysis of *The Nanny* and *La tata* concerns a comparison of Jewish and regional Italian expressions in the dialogue. The first episode of the third season, "The Pen Pal," offers a fundamental example of the linguistic aspects of the adaptation. Fran's mysterious pen pal, Lenny, is finally visiting New York and wants to meet her. Worried about his possible disappointment in a real encounter with her, Fran is extremely nervous and pays particular attention to how she looks. While she is still upstairs getting ready for her date, Maxwell and Niles have a conversation about Fran in which the two British men try to speak Yiddish in the U.S. version, and use expressions from the Naples dialect in the Italian version:

Maxwell: Where is Miss Fine anyways?
Niles: She's upstairs getting all *fapitzed*.
Maxwell: What does that mean?
Niles: You know, dressed.
Maxwell: I thought that was *flubunged*.
Niles: No, Sir, that means confused.
Maxwell: No, man, that's *fechachda*.
Niles: Well, then, what's *flishimeld*?
Maxwell: I think that's her uncle.

Italian version
Maxwell: La signorina Francesca e' scesa?
Niles: Come dicono in Ciociaria, e' su che si *pitta*.
Maxwell: Che cosa fa?
Niles: Si trucca, si pitta.
Maxwell: Non dicono si *dipinge*?
Niles: No signore, quello e' Raffaello.
Maxwell: No, Raffaello non si pittava.
Niles: Neanche andando dal Papa?
Maxwell: No, era Giulio II . . .
Niles: E non voleva?

Literal translation
Maxwell: Is Miss Francesca ready?
Niles: As they say in Ciociaria, she's upstairs and she's *pittando*.
Maxwell: What is she doing?
Niles: She is putting on makeup, *si pitta*.
Maxwell: Don't they say *si dipinge*?
Niles: No sir, that was Rafael, *painting*.
Maxwell: No, Rafael *non si pittava*.
Niles: Not even when he used to meet the pope?
Maxwell: No, it was Julius II.
Niles: And he didn't want him to?

The significant use of Yiddish by two British men stresses Fran's influence in their lives and in the family's life in general, because it is clear that Maxwell and Niles (as well as the kids in other episodes) have assimilated the nanny's linguistic heritage and, with that, her Jewishness. In the Italian version Maxwell and Niles undergo a similar linguistic transformation. The two men, in fact, use expressions from Fran's dialect, but the conversation is based not only on linguistic jokes, but also on traditional Italian cultural stereotypes. Maxwell and Niles mention the painter Rafael and Pope Julius II, and play with the double meaning of the words *pittare* and *dipingere*, which denote *makeup* and *painting* in the Neapolitan dialect and in "proper" Italian, respectively. This scene in the adaptation of *The Nanny* exemplifies quite well those characteristics of dubbing that allow a text to undergo drastic changes, becoming, to some extent, an entirely *new* product. Again, southern Italy is juxtaposed to the more "proper" and sophisticated Italy through a "simple" juxtaposition of terms. The joke (which in the end does not come out as convincing or comical as the original dialogue in Yiddish) lies in highlighting the difference between Fran's regional *pittare* (considered in its more casual connotation of putting on makeup) and Rafael's standard Italian *dipingere* (considered in its more noble significance of painting).

Accents as well as dialectical and regional expressions are elements that also profoundly influence the modifications made to the original text. Dubbing, therefore, offers a form of manipulation that depends on several factors that, when combined, may create a version significantly different from the original. Dubbing's potential to change the text introduces interesting questions about *authenticity*, as well as about the broader idea of *authorship* in terms of translation and adaptation. Is the new version an entirely new product as well as a new *text*? Such questions aim to understand if adaptations offer not only a different program but also a different perception and interpretation of it. According to Ascheid, the dubbed version is an original text, and issues of authenticity are "meaningless" since the "dubbed motion picture becomes a new and fundamentally recontextualized product in the process."[21] Hence the thorny debate about the translators' frustration at not being considered authors. As mentioned in the previous chapter, national associations of dubbing such as AIDAC generally complain about the lack of consideration given to the creative elements introduced by translators in adaptations.

The comparison of *The Nanny* and *La tata* offers a good example in this respect. The adaptation is not only modified in some of its linguistic elements, but also introduces significant cultural and religious differences through changes in the dialogue. In order to maintain the "erasure of Jewishness" as coherent, the Italian translation transforms Fran and her family from Jewish to Catholic. Given the massive influence of the Catholic Church and the Vatican in Italian life, it is not surprising that the adaptation tries to recreate a familiar religious environment. Such a fundamental change from the original version causes the dialogue to undergo drastic modification, especially in relation to the visual presence of Jewish elements in the series, such as Fran and Sylvia attending synagogue in "The Cantor Show" or the rabbi and Jewish guests in the wedding episode. Although the series has to deal with Jewish visual elements on many occasions (given the importance of the New York/Jewish stereotypes in the U.S. version), these two particular episodes illustrate and exemplify the problems of the translation in attempting to rationalize the new Catholic environment of the Italian version.

"The Cantor Show," an episode from the third season, shows Fran attending synagogue and dating the new cantor, who later will be contracted by Maxwell as the main singer for his latest Broadway production. The translation needs to justify Fran's and Sylvia's presence in the synagogue in the first place, and the solution is found by having the two women attending the service with a Jewish cousin they mention but who is never shown on screen. When Fran and Gary, the cantor, speak for the first time, Fran makes jokes about Jewish traditions in Italian (while in the original version she lies about her age) and shows a clear ignorance about religious matters (she confuses the synagogue with a mosque). The translation, therefore, adds cultural and religious elements not originally present in the dialogue. Dubbing, then, not only detaches Fran from her Jewishness, but also highlights her supposed ignorance about any "foreign" religious traditions. Gary constantly reminds the audience how Fran—a Christian—and he get along despite their different religious beliefs, reconfirming the idea that Fran and her family are "devoted" Italian Catholics. What is missing in comparison with the original version, in fact, is the irony embedded in Sylvia's and Fran's own eccentric interpretation of their religion, which includes eating ham sandwiches in the synagogue and passing them off for turkey sandwiches, or eating pork at Chinese restaurants because "it doesn't count if it's Chinese." Part of Fran's (and Sylvia's) stereotypical portrayal as Jewish in the U.S. version, in fact, strongly relies on jokes and self-irony about Judaism and the breaking of many religious rules, a factor that adds to the eccentricity of Fran's family. As exemplified by "The Cantor Show," whenever jokes about religion are maintained in the Italian adaptation, they never really refer to Catholicism. This drastic change from the original version aims to create an environment familiar to an audience used to the strong influence of the Catholic Church in many aspects of daily life, but it also explains the traditional tendency of Italian network executives to erase religious differences and jokes. As Corizza explains:

> Up to at least ten years ago talking about different religions or mock-ing the Catholic Church was not common on television. Now we can play more with it, but in the 1990s it was unthinkable. Thus, we thought about domesticating Fran more in a folkloric way as a *paesana*, instead of heavily relying on religion.[22]

In this respect, the episode in which the original version undergoes the most significant changes (and is perhaps less credible because of the presence of unavoidably problematic visual elements) is Fran and Maxwell's wedding episode, aired at the end of the fifth season. The U.S. version shows a mixed wedding (Jewish and Christian) celebrated both by a rabbi and an Anglican pastor. The Italian version transforms the original mixed wedding into a Catholic civil ceremony, where the pastor, turned into a Catholic priest, administers the rite together with an improbable justice of the peace (the rabbi in the U.S. version). This choice, then, not only shows how Fran's Jewish beliefs are erased and domesticated into the Catholic faith, but also illustrates how Maxwell's religion is ignored and made invisible (since the person administering the rite is not a religious figure, but a justice of the peace). The signifi-cance of the Catholic Church is thus highlighted on multiple levels, by both domesticating and erasing religious differences.

The major problems in this adaptation, however, were in justify-ing the presence of clearly Jewish guests at the ceremony, as well as the performance of the traditional "Hava nagila" dance for the bride and groom during the wedding party. These visual aspects could not really be adapted and appear in the Italian version as purely traditional and picturesque rituals detached from any religious significance. As men-tioned above, this episode is not particularly credible and effective in its adaptation, given the multiple *visual* elements that ultimately cannot be modified; the audience is left, in the end, with unanswered questions about the Jewish elements in the mise-en-scène and a general sense of disorientation and alienation from the text.

Although it presents several problems, this episode also supports the idea that translators are authors, and the linguistic and cultural elements modified in the adaptation, do indeed create new texts. The translators' desire to be considered authors appears to be, in this respect, legitimate, because in the final instance it is their work that allows the effective perception and understanding of a text in its new context.

Concluding Remarks: Matzah Balls? I'd Rather Have Meatballs

The Nanny certainly represents an extreme case of textual manipulation obtained through the use of dubbing, which "recreates" a series in a way that is closer to a "remake" than to "traditional" audiovisual translation. The analysis of the Italian version of *The Nanny* shows how, despite the general tendency toward media globalization, imported formats undergo drastic processes of modification in order to become more comprehensible and appealing to their new audience. The use of regional expressions and popular humor, made possible thanks to the multifaceted characteristics of dubbing, allow national elements and stereotypes to be explored and reinforced. *The Nanny* and its adaptation highlight the necessity for cultural specificity in translating imported programs, and represent an interesting example of how network television in Italy constantly employs national stereotypes based on the idea of the North/South division.

The translation of *The Nanny* also testifies to the problems that dialogue writers confront when they make certain changes once a series is first imported and then have to adapt the rest of the episodes to resonate both with those modifications as well as with the progression of the original story line. An unanswered question is whether the Italian audience would have understood the original series and its Jewish irony without any modifications, a possibility that calls into question Mediaset's ultimate goals for such changes. But perhaps not: *The Nanny* aired from 1995 to 2001 on Mediaset's Italia 1 channel under the title of *La tata* and brought about the creation of "*La tata* Fans Club," founded in 1998. The series was particularly successful because of the sympathy it generated among Italians who identified with the eccentric "Italian" nanny. Although the Italian fan club's Web site explains how Fran's origin was changed from Jewish to southern Italian, fans and commentators on the blog still refer to her as an "Italian."

In November 2002, more than a year after the series ended in Italy, Fran Drescher appeared as a special guest on the Italian TV show *Matricole e meteore* (Freshmen and Shooting Stars), also broadcast on Mediaset. This event not only demonstrated the continued affection of Italian audiences for the actress and her character, but also introduced further complexities. Drescher appeared on Italian television supposedly to teach the audience how to cook meatballs in marinara sauce, a traditional Italian American dish. Her live appearance in Italy confirmed the changes introduced in the Italian adaptation, since the original Jewish American setting was not mentioned at all and Drescher's ehtnic cooking reinforced the idea of her as a perfect Italian-style nanny. What happened on *Matricole e meteore* illustrates how Drescher and the other producers of *The Nanny* must have known about the changes made to the Italian version, and thus, were aware that the main Jewish comic elements of the series had been lost. Corizza confirms this idea and finds justification in the fact that the Jewish American stereotype simply has no correspondence in Italy. Therefore, changes were necessary first in order to have the Italian network buy the series, and then to have the new audience relate to the characters.[23] Thus, indigenized versions of globally distributed programs become more profitable both for the original American networks and the foreign importers.

This example invites us to consider the "artistic compromises" authors such as Fran Drescher are willing to accept when they try to export a product abroad. The analysis of the audience becomes in this respect particularly interesting. Further research can be dedicated to the study of spectators and their identification with the character, and whether the Italian audience ultimately identifies with Fran (or Francesca) because of her humor and eccentric kindness or because she is "Italian." The adaptation of *The Nanny* can ultimately be seen as a challenge to and reaction against the increasing tendency toward media globalization, although it was made, of course, in hopes of large profits. What comes across in the adaptation are those North versus South stereotypes on which Italian humor has traditionally been based. It can be argued, in fact, that the new version of the series does not effectively reinforce Italian cultural identity as a whole, but rather perpetrates the incommensurable divide between the South and the rest of Italy in the name of a "better" (and more profitable) understanding of the final product.

If this tendency toward the exploitation of cultural specificity on television for economic purposes is already clear in the case of *The Nanny,* the following chapter's discussion about *The Simpsons* further illustrates the network executives' interest in adapting global programs for local sales. In fact, while *The Nanny's* American producers simply accepted and supported the changes made to the series in order to sell it in Italy, Fox and Gracie Films (coproducers of *The Simpsons*) went so far as to get directly involved in the choice of translators and dubbing actors abroad to ensure sales in foreign markets.

CHAPTER FOUR

Dubbing *The Simpsons:*
Or How Groundskeeper Willie
Lost His Kilt in Sardinia

"Hi-diddly-ho, neighbors!"
How the hell are they going to translate that?
A *SIMPSONS* FAN ON A BLOG

A Worldwide Look at *The Simpsons*

The above epigraph refers to the difficulties of trying to translate the childlike expressions of Homer Simpson's neighbor Ned Flanders in dubbing *The Simpsons* for foreign audiences. More specifically, however, the epigraph voices the reaction of a disappointed Arab fan of *The Simpsons* after he discovered that the cult animated series was going to be adapted and made more "appropriate" for Arab audiences.[1]

In September 2005, almost sixteen years after *The Simpsons* premiered as a half-hour series in the United States, the Arab network MBC (based in Dubai Media City) introduced Homer & Co. to the Middle East.[2] Given the international popularity of the show from the 1990s to the present, one might assume that *The Simpsons* does not require significant changes when exported abroad because of the familiarity that audiences worldwide have with the characters. Executives at MBC, however, felt that the Arab world needed a version of *The Simpsons* more in line with the feelings and beliefs of Islam, and thus they launched an "Arabized" hybrid of the series called *Al Shamshoon.* Thus, MBC altered the original text by changing some elements of the show through the Arab voice-over. As a consequence, just as Fran Drescher, the Jewish protagonist of *The Nanny,* becomes Italian American for Italian audiences, similarly Homer Simpson becomes "Omar Shamshoon" for his Arab viewers.

Further, eating habits change accordingly: hot dogs become Egyptian beef sausages, donuts are turned into Arab cookies called *kahk,* and, most unexpectedly, the renowned and omnipresent Duff beer is watered down to become simple soda.[3]

While the idea of a sober Homer certainly seems an outrageous offense to *Simpsons* aficionados, such changes are not surprising given the circumstances of programming in which they came about: among other things, *Al Shamshoon* premiered on MBC during Ramadan, a time of both high television ratings and profound cultural and religious significance for the Arab world.[4] This case is a particularly revealing example of how television executives aim at making a foreign product familiar (and "proper") so as to appeal to domestic audiences and maximize profit. MBC's adaptation of *The Simpsons,* in fact, is only one instance of the many transformations the series has undergone through the years when it has been exported abroad. Indeed, if audiences worldwide are familiar with the yellow animated characters from Springfield, most likely it is because they have watched a dubbed or subtitled version of the show, and not because they have been exposed to the original episodes in English. The importance given to the translation of *The Simpsons* is confirmed by the attention that Fox and Gracie Films (coproducers of the series) have paid to every phase of the show's international distribution. As Marion Edwards, executive vice president of international television at Fox, reveals in an interview with the author, the two production companies have been directly involved in the choice of translators and voice-over actors in most of the countries where the series has been exported. In Italy, in particular, Gracie Films has worked in collaboration with Mediaset (the local distributor of *The Simpsons*) to find voices for dubbing that would match those of the original American actors as closely as possible. Further, Gracie Films was directly involved in the choice of the Italian translator for the series.[5]

Such close attention to the exported product is explained, first of all, by the large economic interest both Fox and Gracie Films have in the success of *The Simpsons* abroad. Through merchandizing and DVD sales, *The Simpsons* remains one of the most profitable shows on U.S. television, so the involvement of the original U.S. production companies in its international distribution is not surprising. What complicates the matter, however, is the fact that the animated series created by Matt Groening is a product so rich in cultural and political references specific to the United States that great creativity and professionalism are mandatory for achieving a successful translation. Cultural content is so relevant that, at times, even small visual details can create problems in foreign markets. Marion Edwards explains, for example, how the show received a cold welcome when first exported to Japan because all the characters in the series have four fingers. *Variety* reports how "having fewer than five digits in Japanese culture could signal a lower-class status (as in a butcher's occupational hazard), and thus a tough-sell to glamour-loving Japanese auds."[6] Further, Bart's disrespectful attitude toward his parents and every other authoritarian figure has also been difficult to sell in Asian countries, where respect for one's elders is a given cultural tradition. The solution found at Fox, in this case, was to market *The Simpsons* in Asia focusing on Lisa's intellectual character instead of Bart's more "hip" attitude.[7]

These examples, together with that of MBC's *Al Shamshoon,* support once again the idea that translations are bridges not only between different languages, but also between different cultures. Further, audiovisual translations do not only modify the actual text: considered in a broad sense, they also provoke a systematic reorganization of programming and marketing strategies, a process that in itself represents a form of translation.

On this basis, the Italian translation of *The Simpsons* is an adaptation that involves not only linguistic and cultural factors but also aspects of programming. The modifications that have followed the logics of distribution, far from depriving the show of its humor, have allowed the series to become particularly successful in Italy. This chapter explores some of the changes made to the program, and poses the following questions regarding the strategies employed to make *The Simpsons* more appealing to Italian audiences: (1) How does the translation of *The Simpsons* modify the characters and recontextualize its archetypical and stereotypical features within a national framework of reference? (2) How does the translation reproduce the ethnic and racial multiplicity of *The Simpsons* within Italy's borders? And more generally, (3) How does Italian television translate and adapt the many cultural references in *The Simpsons* so as to recreate the show's humor, satire, and irony? These particular questions arise when one realizes that in the many adaptations of *The Simpsons* abroad, two main elements emerge that, when "indigenized," increase the show's appeal: its references to popular culture and the stereotypical depiction of the characters. Italy is no exception in this respect: the translation relocates most of the cultural allusions to a new national (Italian) context and re-territorializes the characters according to domestic stereotypes.

What is most interesting and challenging in an analysis of *The Simpsons* is the fact that the show has been strongly identified with postmodern America, and praised for its pungent and precise satire of contemporary American society. How, then, can it be localized for other parts of the world? Duncan Stuart Beard discusses the Americanness of the show, focusing on the difficulties involved in the translation of a type of satire "whose intent is locally directed."[8] Beard examines *The Simpsons* to consider what happens when satire travels abroad and risks getting lost in translation:

> What the satirical elements of *The Simpsons* are ultimately involved in is an analysis of American socio-cultural practices and their relation to American notions of American identity. It is when viewed in this manner that its satire is at its most effective. Its interrogation of American identity assumes what is, for American audiences, an intuitive understanding of unspoken (and unspeakable) issues, primarily concerning what it means to be American.[9]

Although *The Simpsons* is undoubtedly rooted in specific references to American culture, Beard also argues that the show is successful worldwide because it manages to go beyond the constraints of its specific local irony. In particular, Beard contends, "what *The Simpsons* presents is not a form of global culture, but of local culture with a global reach." He argues that *The Simpsons* is popular at home for its local satirical elements and successful abroad for the global themes and stereotypes it presents, and ultimately "works best in directing its satiric energies against that mass media that is so often seen as threatening us with an increasingly homogenized cultural experience."[10]

Expanding on Beard's analysis, this chapter argues that *The Simpsons* is successful abroad not only for its global reach, but also for the possibilities it offers for recontextualization and local adaptation for foreign markets. In other words, what makes *The Simpsons* particularly popular worldwide are the many adaptations it has undergone that have "indigenized" the text for foreign audiences.

The Italian translation of *The Simpsons*—*I Simpson*—is an all-encompassing process that includes changes to the characters' names and accents, acronyms, jokes, catchphrases, cultural references, signs, billboards, advertising jingles, songs, and episode titles. All the changes included in the translation of the series testify to the efforts made by the network (through the translator and the dialogue writer) to domesticate the program for Italian audiences. In this respect, the Italian adaptation of *The Simpsons* becomes particularly creative in its depiction of the show's secondary characters. The series is filled with minor figures that represent the entire population of Springfield in all its idiosyncrasies and stereotypical institutional roles: the reverend, the chief of police, the school principal, the bartender, and others. While the original U.S. voice-overs tend to play more with the tone of the characters' voices, often inspired by the famous actors and actresses who play them, the Italian translation adds regional accents to the characters, re-territorializing them across Italian geographical and stereotypical lines. As Francesca in *La tata* lives in Manhattan but is turned into an Italian American, *I Simpson* is still based in Springfield and the characters are still "Americans." However, having the characters speak with various Italian accents corresponds to specific cultural stereotypes and represents a conscious effort to indigenize and domesticate the series for distribution in Italy.

The following sections explore the significance of these modifications, from the domestication of the ethnic attributes of the characters to the adaptation of the many cultural references in the series. The goal is to trace a direct correspondence between the efforts made toward indigenization and interest in maximizing profits from the series' distribution in Italy.

Global Reach Versus Local Appeal: A Few Generic Considerations

The discussion concerning the domestication of some of the show's characters in the Italian adaptation of *The Simpsons* requires a brief introduction about the role of these characters in the original U.S. version. This will bring in issues of genre that are worth exploring. Establishing the generic nature of *The Simpsons* and Fox's original idea about its intended audience is important in order to understand the corresponding Italian conception about the program and its targeted audience.

It has been argued extensively that *The Simpsons* is stylistically and generically a combination of animation and family sitcom. The argument in favor of animation is fairly straightforward—*The Simpsons* is indeed an animated series. The idea of the show as a sitcom, however, might not be as obvious. Communication scholar Megan Mullen traces the origins of *The Simpsons* back to Hanna-Barbera's cartoons (*The Flintstones* and *The Jetsons*), the magicoms of the late 1960s (*Bewitched* and *I Dream of Jean-*

nie), and the working-class and "socially relevant" sitcoms (*The Honeymooners, All in the Family,* and *Roseanne,* among others).[11] The series' similarity with *The Flintstones* and *The Jetsons* certainly depends on its use of animation to convey irony, but also rests on the legacy of these earlier animated series and the decision to air them during prime time, as well as their marketing more as family sitcoms made for adults rather than for children.[12] Mullen clarifies these influences on *The Simpsons:*

> The creators of *The Flintstones* and *The Jetsons* had exploited the unique potential of animation as a device to convey irony in an innocuous way, a strategy inherited and further developed by *The Simpsons'* creators decades later. While the sitcom genre itself offers a way to pack stories about common human experiences into less than thirty minutes, animation eliminates any need to meet expectations of verisimilitude. As with children's cartoons, viewers approach these "adult" cartoon sitcoms with suspended disbelief, and in the process absorb significant social commentary.[13]

The kind of witty humor and cultural critique that characterize *The Simpsons* clearly testifies to Fox's intention to target a more adult audience, despite the choice of animation as the stylistic and narrative mode. The schedule of programming in which *The Simpsons* originally aired provides further evidence that the series was considered a sitcom and not merely a children's cartoon. Indeed, Fox scheduled *The Simpsons* in direct competition with NBC's *The Cosby Show*, which, although in decline when *The Simpsons* premiered, had been one of the most popular family sitcoms on American television.[14]

Among the various elements that define *The Simpsons* as a sitcom, there is one factor that is particularly relevant for the analysis of the indigenization of the series: the presence of an innumerable cast of minor characters, who participate in the development of the story in very significant ways. Horace Newcomb closely examines the dramatic function of the secondary characters in traditional sitcoms and argues that their role goes beyond that of mere foils:

> The supporting characters live somewhere between the improbable world of the central characters and the world as most of the audience experiences it. . . . These supporting characters serve a crucial function in that they stand, dramatically, closer to the value structure of the audience than to that of the central characters.[15]

In this respect, *The Simpsons* not only follows the conventions of traditional sitcoms, but it also expands their possibilities to the extreme. Newcomb's analysis, in fact, could not be truer for *The Simpsons,* whose number of secondary characters is much higher than in live-action sitcoms. Don Payne, writer and co-executive producer of *The Simpsons,* explains how some of the secondary characters were developed during *The Tracey Ullman Show,* where *The Simpsons* originally aired as a series of thirty-second animated shorts. Other characters, however, were created when the series premiered as an autonomous program in 1989, and others were added even later in following seasons. Payne contends that part of the longevity of the show is indeed based on the many secondary characters. First of all, they rise at times to the role of protagonists, therefore introducing alternative narrative into the overall family plot. Second, the minor characters are defined by very specific stereotypical traits that can provide quick and recurrent jokes whenever needed. Payne confesses, in fact, that writers for *The Simpsons* "certainly embrace cultural stereotypes."[16]

Given the variety and number of characters, then, *The Simpsons* is able to explore most of the social and cultural types with which the audience is familiar. The series portrays a greedy and obnoxious boss (Mr. Burns), a corrupt mayor (Quimby), an incompetent chief of police (Wiggum), an immigrant who fights for his rights as a citizen (Apu), a reverend more interested in material goods than in spiritual guidance (Lovejoy), and so on. Clearly enough, these are figures with whom viewers deal on a daily basis, and whose attitudes reflect our own attitudes or remind us of someone we know. In addition, these characters are not only depicted in their respective institutional roles in society; they are also strongly defined by specific social, cultural, and ethnic stereotypes, whose significance is increased by the precise environment—small-town America—in which they function.

The importance of the secondary characters is increased by the fact that the central figures of the show—mainly Bart and Homer—often come out as particularly "improbable" for their exaggerated lack of discipline (Bart) and lack of intelligence and common sense (Homer). As Newcomb contends, "[The central characters] are, in some way, out of touch with our day-to-day sense of how things happen, with the set of laws that allows us to predict the outcome of our actions."[17] The protagonists, therefore, do not usually provide the more realistic solutions to the problems that the audience is likely to have experienced in their own lives.

In this respect, something should be clarified about the central characters in *The Simpsons* and their narrative roles. Accepting the idea that Bart, at first, and later Homer have been considered the main characters of the show, something must be said about their identity in relation to the plot. As Brian Ott argues:

> Bart's identity privileges image over narrative. In contrast to Lisa, Bart has no political commitments and subsequently he can stand against anything. Bart offers a prepackaged image of rebellion, an identity largely independent of the show's weekly narratives.[18]

Similarly, Jerry Herron contends, "[Bart] has no history to bind him to a particular race or class or ethnicity, so he is semiotically up for grabs, and up for grabbing opportunities that await us all."[19] Bart, with his easy catchphrases, his highly visual presence, and his detachment from any specific ethnic, racial, or political identity, represents that "global reach" and appeal that Duncan Stuart Beard discusses. In this respect then, age or generational diversity seems to sell better globally than ethnic diversity, as it is clear how Bart appeals to audiences across lines of age, gender, race, and ethnicity (perhaps with the exception of East Asia, as discussed in the introductory paragraphs). The audience laughs at the disastrous outcomes of Bart's actions because they often entail and produce slapstick comedy that is not based on his ethnic identity, but rather on his "age identity" as a disrespectful kid. A way to indigenize Bart, therefore, is through the localization of his actions, which can become very culturally specific, even if not related to a particular ethnic or political identity. An interesting example of this type of indigenization is the voice-over that translates Bart's punishments in the opening credits of each episode. The punishment always consists of having Bart write on the school blackboard a different repeated phrase that corresponds to the action done in class—action for which he has been punished in the first place. Bart's rebellious personality is introduced right in the credits, since the audience is presented each show with a different form of insubordination that causes him to stay after class. As indicated earlier, the original U.S. version has Bart write (in English) on the board, with no need for voice-over to explain what he is writing. The Italian version, however, maintains the original visuals, but has the voice-over "translate" what is on the board for the Italian-speaking audience. Most times this is a translation of what Bart is actually writing, but there are a few instances in which the translation adapts and modifies the action for which Bart is being punished. In the early episode "Bart the Genius," Bart writes, "I won't waste chalk." The wasting of chalk is not too serious an action in itself, but the joke lies in the fact that writing ad nauseam on the blackboard is certainly a waste of chalk, so the punishment makes less sense than the action being punished. The Italian version, however, seems less focused on the preservation of the original joke and more interested in establishing Bart's character as a brat (which is also an anagram of his first name) from the very beginning. The translation changes the cause of the punishment, and while Bart writes, "I won't waste chalk," the voice-over says, "Non disegnero' donne nude in classe" (I won't draw naked women in class), an action much more serious, especially for a ten-year-old. The dubbed version, then, portrays Bart as almost erotically deviant, employing a cultural (global) stereotype often associated with Italians as overtly sensual and sexual. Italian "supposed sensuality," in fact, is stereotypically constructed for Italian audiences as well, and based on a more international idea of Italian-ness than on a truly Italian self-image. Clearly, Bart's indigenization is based less on specific ethnic and regional stereotypes than it is on more general characteristics, which concern Italian-ness in a more global sense. Bart's global reach, indeed, offers translators a fairly easy task when it comes to adapting the character for foreign audiences, as the Italian case demonstrates.

Homer is very similar in this respect, but for different reasons. Ott again provides an insightful explanation:

> [Homer] furnishes a vehicle for endless intertextual reference and exemplifies a radical postmodern multiplicity—"an extreme rejection of boundary, stability, historicity, and any concept of a cohesive self." In essence, Homer models an anti-identity; his being critiques the modernist idea of a unified, coherent subject.[20]

By defying the reassuring idea of a unified subject, Homer's personality becomes hard to fully embrace and, consequently, hard to localize in its social, ethnic, and national individuality. Conversely, Homer's very lack of personal specificity has been a major factor in him becoming such an icon of global popular culture. Certainly several factors make Homer easily "up for global grabs." Like Bart, he is the cause of the slapstick aspects of the show, and also serves as the engine for the improbable complications of the plot. These elements add to his more universal appeal, since the humor is often based on the visuals. In addition, one of the traits that more strongly define Homer's character is his habitual dependence on consumption. Homer is particularly sensitive to deceptive commercial advertising, a factor that often turns into a narrative mechanism that triggers the action. To relate this aspect back to issues of identity, Homer is defined essentially by "what he buys" more than by "what he is" or "what he says" (with the exception of his world-renowned "d'oh!"). A more effective way to localize Homer, then, is through the indigenization of what he purchases, instead of through the way he expresses himself. An example of this strategy is at play in an episode from Season 9, "Lisa's Sax." The Simpson family is having a conversation in the living room when Marge asks Homer to hold Maggie and put her to sleep. Homer thinks that an effective way to get Maggie drowsy is to give her some beer, so he puts the can of Duff in her mouth while crooning, "Come on, Maggie, It's Miller time, it's Miller time." Homer's dialogue recalls both a specific and real brand of beer—Miller—and its renowned American commercials, extolling, "It's Miller time." The real reference, then, is to American popular culture, as the famous commercial tagline was coined in the 1970s and has been repurposed in various forms to this day.[21] One of Homer's most characteristic features is his love for beer; indigenizing this habit, then, is an effective strategy to localize Homer while maintaining his identity intact.

The Italian translator takes the cultural reference into consideration, and looking for an appropriate alternative, has Homer say, "Maggie . . . birra, e sai cosa bevi!" (Maggie . . . beer, and you know what you're drinking!). The catchphrase, easily remembered by any adult in Italy, refers to a popular 1980s commercial in which Neapolitan actor, TV host, and musician Renzo Arbore promoted and guaranteed the quality of Italian beers. While not related to any specific brand, the reference to the beer commercial and what it represents is precise, and targets the same adult audience in both countries. Homer, therefore, becomes "local" in his consumerist traits, which are not based on ethnic, racial, or political factors, but on more global aspects of popular culture. Like Bart's indigenization, Homer's transfer to the Italian context is fairly straightforward and based on comical and cultural characteristics that easily appeal abroad. This is not to say that their characters remain "untouched" when the series is exported, but their indigenization is based less on linguistic and ethnic translation.

In contrast, many of the secondary characters in *The Simpsons* are depicted through their national, racial, and ethnic characteristics and idiosyncrasies, which are more locally specific than Bart's and Homer's attributes. Such specificity is what challenges translators the most, but is also what offers them concrete and creative possibilities for indigenization. In this respect, Beard points out the importance of such secondary characters to the original U.S. version, but he also argues that their portrayal has created several problems when the series was exported abroad:

> The eccentric cast of characters who constitute *The Simpsons'* heterogeneous vision of the American public provides a solid foundation upon which to base its critique of numerous elements of American life. In regard to the massive success of the show in foreign markets, however, this factor has also created interpretative problems for international audiences, particularly concerning the show's satiric intent.[22]

As Beard observes, what is particularly significant about the importance given to secondary characters is the fact that they represent the kind of society that *The Simpsons* ultimately criticizes. Hence, not only does the series make ironic statements about idiosyncrasies related to institutional and social figures, but it also shows those figures in all their autonomous and precise stereotypical traits.

As mentioned in the introductory section, the Italian adaptation of *The Simpsons* becomes particularly creative and insightful when it re-territorializes these characters and their traits within an Italian frame of reference. This indigenization is achieved mainly through the use of various Italian accents and dialects to dub the show's secondary characters. In so doing, the translation of *The Simpsons* for Italian audiences not only maintains the global appeal of these ironic portrayals (as Beard argues), but it localizes them, transferring the humor to a new national context. For example, considering the influence of the Catholic Church and the common tendency to criticize it, Italians are certainly familiar with religious figures who do not quite play their role as God's ministers, but rather use the church to attain personal benefits (like the show's Reverend Lovejoy). Similarly, many stereotypes in Italy are related to the corruption of politics and the police, and therefore characters such as Mayor Quimby and Chief Wiggum find fertile ground in the Italian context.

Further, given the diversity of regional intonations and corresponding cultural types that Italian society offers, the small town of Springfield is imaginatively transferred to the Mediterranean peninsula fairly easily and effectively. To clarify, *I Simpson* is not geographically transported and based in Italy, but the stereotypical traits of its citizens are. Tonino

Accolla, dialogue writer and director of dubbing for *I Simpson,* confirms and describes the conscious efforts made to depict the characters in terms of certain stereotypes. As he contends, this goal is often achieved in Italy through the use of regional accents: "In *I Simpson* I used many different accents. Accents from Chieti, from Venice, from Naples, from Calabria. Accents in Italy immediately recall precise personalities."[23] In this respect, Accolla's comments fit particularly well with Antje Ascheid's theorization about the "rewriting" of new characters through dubbing: "These new characters are uttering a translated, which always also means interpreted, appropriated, and re-created new text, thus undergoing fundamental shifts in the construction of their national and cultural identity and context."[24]

Indigenizing Characters: Accents, Stereotypes, and the "Others"

Writing about the translation of *The Simpsons* in France, sociolinguist Nigel Armstrong claims that "the relative leveling of French pronunciation puts difficulties in the way of the oral translation of some social-regional accents that are used with rather subtle effect in *The Simpsons.*"[25] While not entirely judging the value of the translation per se, Armstrong's study examines the effectiveness of the adaptation of *The Simpsons* from English into French. His examples show how the lack of a wide variety of accents in the French language creates difficulties in attempts to localize the program, because the many accents of the original dialogue cannot be properly transferred into the French context.[26]

In this respect, the Italian case is opposite to that of the French case. Italy offers a greater range of accents and inflections than does the United States, and therefore the translator is presented with several possibilities for indigenizing the text. The Italian translation, in fact, not only reproduces the use of accents in the American version in a new national and regional context, but it also adds accents where they were not originally present. The result is a picturesque community of characters whose linguistic peculiarities increase their appeal for the Italian audience. What follows are discussions of two groups of secondary characters from *The Simpsons* who have been linguistically localized. The first group includes those characters (Fat Tony, Moe Szyslak, Otto Mann, and Chief Wiggum) whose indigenization is based on stereotypes and personalities related to the use of Italian regional accents, but which also correspond to the American stereotypes employed to create the original characters. The second group involves linguistic discussion as well, but also includes national, ethnic, and racial factors, since this set of characters (Groundskeeper Willie and Apu Nahasapeemapetilon) presents elements of foreign "Otherness"—those also indigenized so that their "Otherness" is geographically and linguistically transferred and made comprehensible in the Italian context.

Fat Tony, Moe, Otto, and Clancy: Regionalized Characters

ANTHONY D'AMICO (FAT TONY)

Fat Tony is the typical Italian American mobster, a figure that has become popular through the worldwide distribution of the gangster genre. As a consequence, his character is easily recognizable in the United States and abroad because of global exposure to American gangster movies and television series, from the 1930s gangster movies to *The Godfather* saga and, more recently, *The Sopranos*. Fat Tony engages in several criminal activities: from his involvement in the dairy industry that provides rat milk to Springfield Elementary School, passing it off as regular milk ("Mayored to the Mob"), to the forgery of immigration documents that he provides to Apu when the latter is at risk of being deported ("Much Apu About Nothing"). Dubbed by Italian American actor Joe Mantegna in the original series, Fat Tony's voice and tone evoke those of many Italian American gangsters portrayed in the media. The regional accent chosen by the Italian translators for Fat Tony is Sicilian, because it is immediately associated with illegal activities related to the Mafia. The accent, therefore, conventionally associates Fat Tony with the mob, and it is significant here because it demonstrates how the use of southern Italian accents for mobsters is a well-established practice in Italian audiovisual translation.

MOE SZYSLAK

Moe Szyslak is the bartender and owner of Moe's Tavern, Homer's favorite location in Springfield. Moe is characterized, in the original U.S. version, by a consistent ambiguity regarding his downwardly mobile life and his suspect origins. His actions are usually dubious, and few are the instances in which the audience is informed about details of his life. One such example is an episode from Season 7, "Much Apu About Nothing." As I will discuss it more in detail in the analysis of Apu's character, the episode focuses on a referendum proposed by Mayor Quimby for the approval of a new anti-immigration law. In order to remain in the country, Apu must apply for citizenship and take a written and oral exam to prove his knowledge of American history, culture, and politics. In the citizenship classroom, Moe is shown hiding behind a fake moustache taking the test together with Apu and Willie (originally from India and Scotland, respectively). Consequently, we can legitimately assume that Moe is not a legal U.S. citizen.

In the Italian translation Moe is localized on two separate levels. First, his given name is changed from Moe to Boe. While such a change might seem neither relevant nor necessary, it actually represents an interesting and creative way to indigenize the character. The name "Boe" does not exist in Italian, but it sounds like "boh," a very common Italian expression, which means "I don't know." On the one hand, as *The Simpsons* translator Elena Di Carlo reports, the change to Boe is a comical mechanism because Italians use the word "boh" very frequently with amusing nonchalance.[27] On the other hand, given that the audience, indeed, does not know much about the character, Boe turns into a humorous expression that also highlights the character's ambiguity. In addition, Boe occasionally speaks with a Sicilian accent. The fact that he expresses himself with a regionalized inflection (an element not present in the original U.S. version) only in a few episodes also increases his ambiguity. Through the choice of his first name and his occasional localization as a Sicilian, the Italian translation highlights Moe/Boe's tendency to hide information about his life, which is the most distinctive trait of the character in the original U.S. version. The indigenization, therefore, ultimately aims at recreating an impression about the character similar to that of the American series.

OTTO MANN

Otto Mann is the school bus driver, whose "stoner" incompetence and lack of any sense of responsibility often get him into trouble. Otto incarnates a "slacker" version of the "Peter Pan syndrome"; he is a twenty-nine-year-old male who lacks ambition, and only wants to play the guitar (this last attribute is highlighted in Italian by a change to his last name from Mann to Disc). The Peter Pan stereotype is well translatable in Italy to the figure of *mammone* (mama's boy). One of the most recurrent jokes about Italian men (in Italy and abroad) concerns their inability to leave the home and care of their parents, especially their mothers. Although not particularly dependent on his parents, Otto presents some of the characteristics and stereotypical traits of those young adults who refuse responsibility, much like the *mammone*. The stereotype associated with *mammone* does not depend on particular regional traits, but is spread throughout the peninsula. The Italian writers, however, chose a Milanese accent for Otto's voice-over. The choice of this accent adds humor to the depiction of the character, not because Otto fits the cultural stereotype associated with Milan, but because he contradicts it completely. Milan is the most industrialized and residential city in Italy, thus the Milanese stereotype is of people who are snobbish, pretentious, ambitious, and very efficient. Otto could not be further from this description. The humor and irony, then, lie in setting expectations through the use of a specific accent that evokes a certain regional type, and then challenging those same expectations with a character who contradicts them all.

CLANCY WIGGUM

Clancy Wiggum is Springfield chief of police. He is overweight, a factor highlighted by an enormous belly, and his character is defined by his continual eating, incompetence, lack of intelligence, and corrupt practices. In the original U.S. version, the voice-over actor plays with Wiggum's voice in an imitation of actor Edward G. Robinson. A Jewish immigrant from Romania, Robinson became hugely popular for his portrayal of Italian American gangster Little Caesar in the 1931 film of the same name.[28] In the U.S. version the irony is based on the use of a generic "funny" voice (for a young and less educated audience) and, more specifically, on the parody of Edward G. Robinson (for older and more cultured viewers).

In Wiggum's case, the Italian translation is particularly creative and effective. The character's last name is changed from Wiggum to Winchester, after the famous rifle and shotgun brand, to mock American police officers' ease with weapons. The Italian voice-over actor dubbing Wiggum also speaks with a marked Neapolitan accent, which conventionally makes the character sound amusing. The Neapolitan accent, in fact, is particularly loved in Italy and, as Milly Buonanno contends, theater, film, and television have traditionally accustomed Italians to associate the Neapolitan accent and dialect with comedy.[29]

In addition to speaking with a Neapolitan *accent*, Wiggum's jargon is also strongly based on the Neapolitan *dialect*. The chief of police usually addresses criminals as *guaglio'* (short for *guaglione*), one of the most authentically Neapolitan expressions, translatable as "kid." Finally, his corrupt practices as a policeman evoke common labels associated with organized crime in Naples, therefore Wiggum fits the characteristics of Neapolitan stereotypes on multiple levels. His accent, the specific words he uses, and the conventional portrayal of Neapolitan police as corrupt imaginatively re-territorialize Wiggum within the Italian context and symbolically "send" the Italian audience home.

Willie and Apu: Diversity, Italian Style

WILLIE: NATIONAL "OTHER"

Willie is the groundskeeper at Springfield Elementary School (and is commonly referred to as "Groundskeeper Willie"). He is usually solitary and aggressive, and he often mentions his rural upbringing in Scotland, his native country. The fact that he is Scottish is highlighted both linguistically and visually. Willie, in fact, speaks with a marked Scottish accent and often wears a kilt. Both elements place Willie as an outsider in Springfield, and he is often the target of jokes planned by the kids in school.

What needs to be re-created in the Italian translation are Willie's Scottish-ness and his alienation from the Springfield community, which speaks and acts differently from the groundskeeper. In this regard, the fundamental difficulty that the Italian translator and dialogue writer encountered was the fact that the Scottish stereotype in Italy does not correspond to the characteristics that Willie presents. Scottish people are considered, in the Italian imaginary, as greedy and particularly prone to drinking. While the Italian idea about Scots might somehow "justify" Willie's aggressive attitude, it does not justify Willie's constant references to his rural lifestyle, which Italians do not associate with Scotland.

The solution chosen involves a drastic transfer of Willie's stereotypical (Scottish) character to a similar cultural personality in Italy who possesses the same characteristics and idiosyncrasies as Willie. Willie becomes, in fact, an immigrant from Sardinia, one of the two Italian island regions. Although Sicily, the other Italian island, is more integrated in the national imaginary, both because of the Mafia and the media (through movies, television fiction, and the news), Sardinia still remains isolated in the stereotypical view of Italians, and is seen as very rural and almost "primitive" (because of the particularly arid nature of its landscapes). In reality, Sardinia is one of the most exclusive and expensive locations for tourism in Italy, attracting thousands of Italians and foreigners every summer, eager to enjoy the beauty of its beaches, the Gennargentu National Park, and many pre-Roman archeological sites. Nonetheless, traditional and stereotypical representation of people from Sardinia, especially in the media, figures a rustic lifestyle and stubborn people usually working as shepherds. In the Italian context, therefore, the Sardinian stereotype fits Willie more appropriately than the Scottish stereotype. Willie as a Sardinian ultimately creates in the Italian audience associations about the character that are analogous to what the American audience associates, knowing that he is Scottish. As for most of the characters, translator Elena Di Carlo reveals that such a change was not made in the actual translation phase, but later, during the adaptation of the dialogue for the screen, by the dialogue writer and director of dubbing as they were rehearsing with the actors.[30] It seems, therefore, that at the level of actual translation, the changes involve primarily the use of specific words, names, and catchphrases. Later, in the subsequent level of adaptation for the screen, the accents come into play to complete the cultural transfer of the characters.

The process of indigenization that Willie undergoes is a significant example of domestication and re-territorialization, and in his case not only on an imaginative level. In the Italian version, in fact, Willie not only speaks with a marked Sardinian accent (as harsh as the Scottish inflection in the U.S. version), but he explicitly comes from Sardinia. With the exception of one ambiguous episode described below, Willie is literally transferred to Italy, geographically, culturally, and linguistically. The ambiguity of Willie's re-territorialization at times creates problems of credibility, but overall it works for the Italian audience, who find in Willie one of their favorite characters, precisely because of his Sardinian accent and temperament.

One of the major obstacles to overcome in the Italian adaptation, however, is visual: Willie often wears a kilt, which is an undeniably Scottish reference. When not ignored in the Italian translation, the kilt is often referred to as a regular skirt and simply considered as an element that adds to Willie's oddity. Overall, then, Willie's wearing a kilt/skirt only increases his strangeness for the Italian audience, but such a trait is usually detached from any national or ethnic aspect of his personality, with the exception of one episode, "Monty Can't Buy Me Love," in which Mr. Burns, Homer, and Willie travel to Scotland, and both Willie and Homer wear kilts (discussed below). Willie's origin from Sardinia is discussed in a few instances in the Italian version, mostly in correspondence to his depiction as Scottish in the U.S. version. Two episodes in the tenth season, in particular, make specific references to Willie as a Scotsman (in the U.S. version) and as a Sardinian (in the Italian version): "Lard of the Dance" and the aforementioned "Monty Can't Buy Me Love." The episodes are interesting because they provide information about Willie, confirming his origin from Scotland in the U.S. version, but creating problems, contradictions, and ambiguity in the Italian translation.

"Lard of the Dance" ("Tanto va Homer al lardo che . . .") is less problematic because every piece of information or joke about Willie is based on language, and therefore fairly easily translatable through dubbing. In the episode, Homer discovers that he can make money by entering the grease-recycling business. After many failed attempts, he decides to steal the school's fat waste with Bart's help. They successfully sneak into the school and start vacuuming the grease out, but Willie discovers them. Homer tries to defend himself by pretending to be an exchange student from Scotland. After hearing that Homer is also Scottish, Willie becomes excited and asks Homer where he is from. Homer replies he comes from "North Kilt Town" and Willie gets even more excited because he comes from the same city and asks Homer if he knows Angus McLeod. The humor of the conversation is further increased by Willie's exaggerated Scottish accent.

The entire dialogue is translated and transferred to the Italian context by substituting every reference to Scotland with a reference to Sardinia. Homer therefore pretends to be an exchange student from Sardinia, hailing from "Nord Pecurone" (literally North Big Sheep Town). Excited, Willie asks if Homer knows Salvatore Udda, and the whole conversation is conducted in strong Sardinian accents. The correspondence between *North Kilt Town* and *Nord Pecurone,* between *Angus McLeod* and *Salvatore Udda,* and between the accents is very precise. In the first case the name of Willie's hometown is based on very stereotypical traits: the kilt for Scotland and the sheep for Sardinia. Similarly, the reference to Angus McLeod and Salvatore Udda is comical because the two names respectively sound undeniably from Scotland and Sardinia. Hence, the conversation is directly transposed into Italian by employing very stereotypical assumptions about Sardinia that correspond to similar assumptions about Scotland. What makes the Italian dialogue even funnier than the American version, however, is the fact that, in translation, Homer starts speaking with a strong accent from Sardinia as well, to better pretend and fool Willie. The consequences of the episode also correspond for the American and Italian audiences: Willie's hometown is confirmed to be in

Scotland (in the U.S. version) and in Sardinia (in the Italian version), even if the names of the two towns mentioned are clearly invented.

A later episode, "Monty Can't Buy Me Love" ("Monty non può comprare amore"), is coherent with "Lard of the Dance" in reestablishing Willie as a Scotsman. However, the Italian version becomes ambiguous because in this episode Willie claims to be born in Scotland as well (as opposed to Sardinia), thus contradicting and confusing all previous information about his character. In the episode, Homer's boss, Mr. Burns, travels to Scotland to look for the Loch Ness monster, capture it, and take it to Springfield in order to finally be loved and appreciated by his fellow citizens. Mr. Burns forces Homer, Willie, and Professor Frink to follow him and help him in the monster's capture. Once at the lakeshore, the professor starts operating complicated machinery to detect the monster in the water, and a curious crowd gathers. Homer notices an older couple in the crowd who resemble Willie quite significantly. Willie confirms that those are his parents, who own a tavern nearby as well as the pool table where he was "conceived, born, and educated." For the American audience, used to hearing Willie speaking with a Scottish accent and seeing him wearing a kilt in Springfield, this episode simply adds information about the character and his comical representation.

The Italian adaptation of this episode presents many challenges for the translators. First of all, the visual references to Scotland are abundant and very explicit, and therefore hard to modify through the voice-over. Second, the older couple shown in the crowd look unquestionably like the groundskeeper, and thus the translation needs to justify the presence of Willie's parents in Scotland even though he speaks with a Sardinian accent. Instead of clarifying information about the character, then, the Italian dialogue increases the ambiguity about Willie. Such difficulties are not isolated cases. These problems arise when choices and changes are made at the time a series is first imported and adapted, and later translators need to be consistent with those initial narrative modifications, even if the visuals contradict them completely. In this case, the challenge is to re-justify Willie's origin from Sardinia even though his family lives in Scotland. The translation changes Willie's origin back to Scotland in this episode, contradicting what previously had been said about his Sardinian origin, but makes every Scotsman in the crowd speak with a Sardinian accent, as if there were a direct—yet imaginative—correspondence between being Scottish and being Sardinian. In addition, right after revealing that he was born in Scotland, Willie makes two precise references to Sardinia that immediately transfer him back to the Italian context. First, once Homer goes underwater to look for the monster and does not reappear on the surface for a while, Willie claims that Homer shows more "stubbornness" than a "goat from Gennargentu," the renowned national park on the east coast of Sardinia. Later in the episode, after Mr. Burns manages to capture the monster by himself, Willie defines him as being "stronger than Gigi Riva." Gigi Riva is a famous retired soccer player, a major star of the Italian national team and leading scorer in the 1970 World Cup, who played for the Cagliari team (the major Sardinian city) for about fifteen years until he retired. Willie's character, therefore, is reconfirmed both as an Italian for his passion for soccer, and ultimately as a Sardinian by making reference to Gennargentu and Riva.

At the risk of falling into a "dangerous" example of self-referentiality that might estrange viewers, the translators needed and opted for two strong narrative reminders that reestablish Willie as a Sardinian. Thus, the importance of both episodes, "Lard of the Dance" and "Monty Can't Buy Me Love," lies in the fact that, against all (visual) odds, Willie is re-territorialized within Italian geography by translating a precise cultural stereotype into a more general Italian one. The Sardinian accent and language sound particularly harsh and therefore represent a good correspondence to the Scottish accent. Linguistically, in fact, the transfer works particularly well because Sardinian (which consists of two major subgroups, Logudorese and Campidanese) is the only idiom in Italy that is not a dialect, but an actual language. Sardinian is autonomous as compared to other modern languages derived from Latin, and is practically incomprehensible to other Italians. Thus, Willie's difficulty in belonging to the community in which he lives is highlighted by the use of an insular idiom, geographically and linguistically detached from mainland Italy. In the translation, therefore, Willie emerges as an outsider, which is ultimately his U.S. role as a Scotsman in Springfield.

APU NAHASAPEEMAPETILON: RACIAL "OTHER"

While Willie presents features that differentiate him from the rest of Springfield in terms of his nationality, Apu Nahasapeemapetilon is represented both as a foreigner and as a racial "Other." Apu is Indian and originally came to the United States to pursue a Ph.D. in computer science. Once in college he began to work at Kwik-E-Mart to pay off his student loans, and never left his convenience store job, even after he received his degree. Apu is married to Manjula, an Indian girl whom his parents chose for him, as is the custom in India. Apu speaks proper English with a strong Indian accent, and maintains his cultural heritage and religious beliefs by displaying in the store a statue of Ganesha, an Indian divinity in the form of an elephant. Apu's representation mixes various common stereotypes associated with Indian immigrants: from being particularly good at engineering and computer science to working twenty-four hours a day in convenience stores. Although racially different from most of the people in Springfield, Apu is generally well accepted in his community, with the exception of one episode, "Much Apu About Nothing," in which he is nearly deported. Mayor Quimby proposes a referendum for the approval of a new law that would force all illegal aliens to leave Springfield and the United States. In order to avoid the possibility of being deported, Apu first turns to the local mobster Fat Tony to provide him with fake documents. When Apu thanks him humbly, Fat Tony promptly replies, "Cut the courtesy, you're an American now!" and suggests that he "act American" if he does not want to look suspicious. As Fat Tony's dialogue reveals, the episode is as much about the stereotypical representation of Apu's Indian heritage as it is about the American lack of tolerance for immigrants. The mocking of the United States becomes more explicit later on in the episode when Homer sees Apu showing off American flags, a cowboy hat, and a New York Mets baseball jersey, as he is now an "American." Apu invites Homer to "take a relaxed attitude for work, and watch the baseball match." Homer is surprised by the changes in Apu, but welcomes the substitution of "that goofy sacred elephant statue" with American magazines in the Kwik-E-Mart. Apu, pretending to agree with Homer, replies, "Who needs the infinite compassion of Ganesha, when I've got Tom Cruise and Nicole Kidman staring at me from *Entertainment Weekly* with their dead eyes?"

In a brief conversation, the writers of the series manage to reduce the United States to a country of cowboys and baseball fans, whose cultural superficiality is highlighted by their reading of Hollywood entertainment magazines. Apu, however, is not only assimilated into the American stereotypical culture of sports and film stars; an additional change Homer notices in Apu, in fact, is in the way he talks. Apu has almost completely erased his Indian accent and awkwardly makes use of American slang such as, "Hey there, Homer, how is it hanging?" Apu, therefore, accepts linguistically and culturally assimilating into American-like language in order to fit into a society that might expel him for his foreignness.

While visually this stereotypical depiction turns out as undeniably comical, hardly hidden behind the humor lies a profound critique of Americans' attitude toward assimilation. Apu's *performed* American-ness is based, in fact, more on appearance and stereotypical symbols of patriotism than on actual manifestations of cultural identity. After all, Fat Tony himself suggests that all Apu has to do it to *act* American—not necessarily *be* American. And it is precisely his performed and arti-ficial identity that soon brings Apu to ultimately reassume his Indian heritage, ashamed at having betrayed his family and roots. He decides, therefore, to take the official test to become a legal citizen and be an American without repudiating his own Indian identity.

Clearly, this episode refers to the 1994 elections in which Californians voted for Proposition 187, a ballot initiative aimed at preventing illegal immigrants from accessing health care benefits and public education. After Apu passes his citizenship exam and Homer is convinced that it is wrong to vote for the new law, Homer organizes a party to celebrate Apu's achievement. Homer makes a speech at the party and claims that many "official Americans" take this country for granted, while immi-grants like Apu are the glue that really holds the society together. De-spite Homer's popularity after his speech, just as Proposition 187 passed in California, so the new law passes in Springfield. As a consequence, many are to be deported—most notably Willie, who closes the episode being forced to leave on a ship (a plot line that is never picked up again). In the meantime, Apu is moved by and cries over receiving a notice for jury duty, considering it a true sign of his new citizenship rights. Soon enough, however, he throws the notice in the trash as an even truer sign of being American.

The episode mocks many stereotypical and problematic American id-iosyncrasies when it comes to immigrants and immigration policy. While the United States has been historically considered a country developed via immigration, Italians have most commonly been known for immi-grating *to* foreign countries, particularly at the turn of the twentieth century. This tendency has changed in the last twenty years as waves of immigrants especially, from North and West Africa, China, Latin Ameri-can, and eastern Europe have begun to move to and settle in Italy. Italy, therefore, has been undergoing a significant change, but the actual full inclusion of immigrants in society is still problematic and controversial. In translation to the Italian context, Apu, and this episode in particular, symbolize the new Italy dealing with immigration issues and struggling to understand its own new identity. The translation has Apu speaking Italian with a marked Indian accent, as in the original. In addition, however, his grammar is poor and his Italian broken and incorrect. Once he tries to pass as a citizen, however, Apu's Italian becomes impeccable and almost without any foreign accent (whereas in the U.S. version, Apu's attempts at "American" English involve him dumbing down his grammar and vocabulary and adopting an over-the-top, John Wayne–type accent). The solution found in the adaptation matches the common stereotype perpetuated in Italy about immigrants who can never really master the national language and can only express themselves in a very limited and comical fashion. With this linguistic choice the Italian translation seems to perpetrate not only a stereotype of exclusion for immigrants but also the idea of Italian superiority, as immigrants are seen as incapable of grasping one of the most elementary aspects of their acquired national identity—language—unless faking it.

Concluding Remarks: We Are Not Racist, We Just Don't Like the South

The idea of national belonging both in the American and Italian examples just described seem to be related to linguistic assimilation, demonstrating once again that language indeed represents a strong marker of cultural and national identity. In this respect, something bears emphasis in the case of Italy. Italians identify themselves primarily along regional as opposed to national lines. Technically, therefore, to really be considered "Italian," foreigners and racial "Others" should be able to assimilate in a regional context, both culturally and linguistically. In this respect, significant is the reaction that Umberto Bossi (the leader of Lega Nord, the right-wing Italian party that promotes Italian regionalism, federalism, and xenophobic sentiments) had in 2003 about voting rights for immigrants. After then–vice prime minister Gianfranco Fini's proposal of a new law that would grant the right to vote to immigrants for municipal elections, Bossi commented that he was going to endorse Fini's proposal only for those immigrants that could speak the *dialect* of the area in which they were going to vote.[31]

The Simpsons and its Italian translation offer an insightful example of this tendency in the character of Carl Carlson. Carl is one of Homer's colleagues at the nuclear power plant. He is an African American who, in the original version, is linguistically integrated within his working and social environment; he was born and raised in the United States and yet represents racial (and, implicitly, gay) diversity. The Italian dialogue writer decided to have Carl speak with a Venetian accent, a factor that both increases the humor and seems to suggest "genuine" belonging. Even if racially diverse from the stereotypical idea of the Italian people, Carl is characterized by a regional inflection, which immediately raises his status to "real Italian." This is different from Apu, who does not speak with any regional inflection and therefore does not really fit in as "Italian." The choice of the Venetian accent for a black character, however, also perpetrates a stereotype of Italian superiority toward immigrants. Federica Bologna hypothesizes about the choice of Carl's accent and argues that the Venetian inflection might depend on historical events. During the Fascist regime before World War II, many unemployed Venetian men were hired by different Italian companies and sent to the Italian colonies in East Africa to teach the natives the job. As a consequence the African people in the colonies not only learned manufacturing skills from the Venetian trainers, but also absorbed their dialect and accents.[32]

The complex representations and linguistic translations of Apu and Carl lie at the core of contemporary debates about who should be "properly" and "officially" considered Italian now that foreign immigrants have started to mix with the white population. An exemplary case of such a debate has been the discussion that divided the media and public opinion in 1996 after the election of Miss Italia. That year, Denny Méndez, a black Latina, won the beauty pageant; originally from the Dominican Republican, she immigrated to Italy after her mother divorced her biological father and married an Italian man. Although Méndez won the popular election of those who were voting from home, the official judges in the competition were divided. There were those who did not consider Méndez's traits and physical characteristics as representing "Italian" beauty. This view championed Sophia Loren and Gina Lollobrigida as true Mediterranean beauties who could legitimately represent Italy and Italian women around the world. The opposing faction argued that Denny Méndez symbolized the real identity of the contemporary Italian population, which was quickly changing. According to this view, Méndez was the face of the new country and was no less Italian than Sophia Loren or any other "proper" Mediterranean beauty.

The controversy over the 1996 election of Miss Italia and the sporadic and very stereotypical, if often derogatory, representations of immigrants on television are central issues that are slowly influencing Italian television executives to support more realistic depictions of foreigners and racial "Others." Since the late 1980s, a few programs on RAI have been produced to sensitize public opinion to immigration issues. Three examples are particularly interesting: *Non solo nero* (Not only black) (1988–1994), *Un mondo a colori* (A world in colors) (1998–2003), and *Shukran* ("Thank you," in Arabic) (1999–present). As communication scholar Michela Ardizzoni contends, the three aforementioned programs "have permanently modified the landscape of Italian television."[33] Yet, similar programming on either RAI or Mediaset (the commercial poles of Italian television) has not bolstered their preliminary efforts.

In terms of televisual representation, in fact, what is more significant is that rarely, if ever, are immigrants figured in national productions of fiction. In other words, *Non solo nero, Un mondo a colori,* and *Shukran* are news programs that inform the audience about concrete issues concerning immigration, but there are almost no corresponding representations of immigrants in television fiction. Giuliano Amato, then minister for internal affairs, highlighted this negligence at the conference on immigration issues, held in Genoa in September 2006. Amato denounced the problematic and almost nonexistent representation of immigrants on Italian television and invited networks executives and producers to create TV fiction that can better and more realistically represent the role of immigrants in contemporary Italy. Significantly, Amato complained that although audiences can see black characters portrayed as doctors or other highly respected professions on American television, on Italian television "we are stuck to representations such as that of Mammy from *Gone with the Wind,* when blacks used to speak like Ciriaco De Mita." Amato refers here to the aforementioned stereotypical depiction of racial "Others" as incapable of mastering the Italian language, a factor that perpetuates the inferiority of immigrants as compared to native— white—Italians. What is even more significant, however, is that Amato compares this supposed linguistic "inability" of foreign immigrants to the common—and highly stereotypical—belief that southern Italians also have difficulties in speaking proper Italian, free from regional expressions or inflections. Ciriaco De Mita, in fact, is an Italian politician from the area surrounding Naples famous for his marked accent and unsophisticated style of public speaking.

Italian racism had manifested itself in the profound division between North and South much before the arrival of foreign immigrants. While acts of racism against racial "Others" in Italy are still frequent, these acts are usually now criticized as unacceptable, and campaigns promoting diversity and multiculturalism have been initiated both at the national and European level. The separation between northern and southern Italy, however, is both accepted and hard to overcome not only because it is rooted in Italian history, but also, and more problematically, because such separation is perpetrated in the stereotypical and often comical representation of southern characters. Thus, ironically, what should be a division to be overcome becomes in reality one of the most successful sources of "humor" on Italian television, whether nationally produced or imported from abroad and dubbed. *The Simpsons* is but one example that confirms this tendency of the Italian media. Most of the characters who have been indigenized through the use of regionalized accents are re-territorialized in the southern areas of Italy. While not all of them are discussed in this study, visually mapping all of these characters within the Italian peninsula gives further evidence of the North-South division and its consequent impact on media representations. Map 4.1 is a map of Italy to which I have added the symbolic origin of the regionalized characters in the Italian version of *The Simpsons* (the line represents the perceived separation between "the North" and the rest of the country).

The map highlights how the geographical distribution of most of the indigenized characters in *The Simpsons* reinforces the idea that southern Italian accents and stereotypes still represent a very common strategy with which to create humor on television. More specifically, the majority of characters re-territorialized in the South are either symbolically from Naples or Sicily, the two areas most profoundly and stereotypically identified with southern Italy. Wiggum's corruption and Fat Tony's mob affiliation, therefore, could not find a more "proper" ground for indigenization, as the recurrent representations and discourses in Italy about the South usually fit these very images—images that repeatedly turn out to be profitable because they are familiar and embedded in the Italian mentality.

The translation of *The Simpsons*, then, exemplifies the tendency of TV networks to use national and cultural stereotypes to re-territorialize characters and the overall narrative according to familiar and profitable patterns. As American writers embrace cultural stereotypes in their creation of the original episodes, so do writers in Italy when they translate them. *The Simpsons* represents a challenge for adaptation because it is deeply rooted in American popular culture, so it is inevitable that comical references are altered and adapted for new audiences. Because of the considerable economic interests involved in the series' merchandising in Italy, additional attention (and money) has been invested in the distribution and dubbing of the series. As a consequence, the original American TV network was actively involved in the processes of transla-

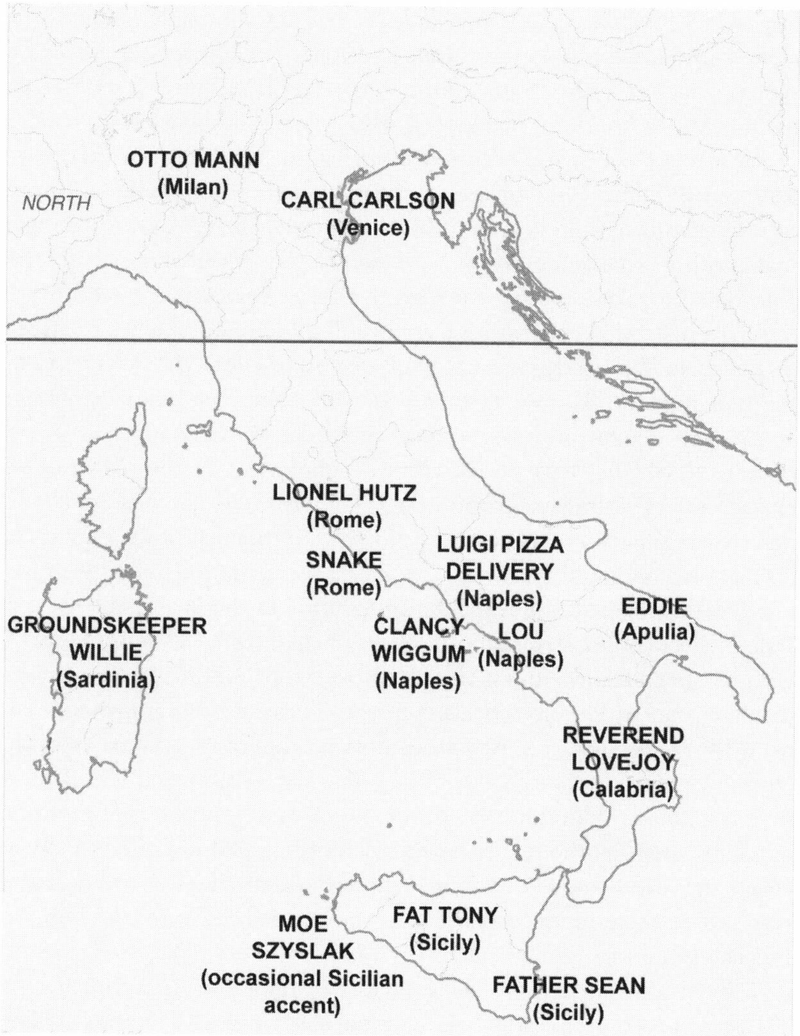

Map 4.1. *The Simpsons'* re-territorialization

tion, dubbing, and adaptation—a situation that rarely occurs in international distribution. In Italy, the particular attention reserved to the series has allowed for all the official and proper phases of dubbing to be respected—a practice not adopted for less profitable shows—from the different professional roles involved to the quality of translation, screen adaptation, voice-over actors, and so forth. The bottom-line is that high quality in translation and dubbing directly depends on the money invested by the original networks and the distribution companies, and such investments clearly depend on the expected profits from both domestic and international sales. For this reason, attention is also dedicated to the particular programming strategies that can more properly and profitably sell a program abroad. Ultimately, the animated nature of *The Simpsons* convinced Italian Mediaset to market the show for children, and to air the program in an afternoon schedule, as animation is not usually "prime-time material" for Italian television. This shift from the original American marketing intent (*The Simpsons* had been targeted to general audiences in the United States, but has progressively shifted toward a more adult type of programming) is significant because targeting the program to a younger audience allowed for massive merchandising sales to children and teenagers, a factor that further justifies the U.S. producers' interest in the reception and marketing of the show in Italy.[34]

Ultimately, therefore, the dubbing of *The Simpsons* as a form of cultural adaptation more than a simple translation, together with strategies of programming, have facilitated the reception of the series in Italy. Overall, *The Simpsons* has been extremely successful and well received in Italy, both because of its global cult status and for the specific national characteristics it has gained in the adaptation. As happens in *The Nanny*, *The Simpsons* becomes more appealing because domesticated and made more familiar in those aspects that might have otherwise seemed foreign to the Italian audience. As explored in the next chapter, however, an opposite strategy needs to be employed at times when a program's themes might be, on the contrary, "too familiar" and therefore problematic or simply not interesting. The adaptation of *The Sopranos*, in fact, balances domestication and foreignization to make the series profitable, but also to avoid troubling references to the Mafia, a subject still very sensitive for Italian media.

CHAPTER FIVE

The Sopranos in Italy: Or "Why Should We Care? We Have the Real Mafia Here!"

Italians find it hard to imagine a mobster seeing a shrink. They just don't get the joke.
GIANNI GALASSI, ON DUBBING *THE SOPRANOS*

Gangsters in Translation

In Chapter 3 I discussed how the sitcom *The Nanny* has been drastically modified and made familiar for Italian audiences by changing the protagonist's ethnic background from Jewish (in the U.S. version) to Italian American (in the Italian version). Similarly, the dubbing of *The Simpsons* (discussed in Chapter 4) domesticates the series for Italian audiences by making references to popular (national) culture and by giving regional accents to some of the characters, thereby mapping them within precise stereotypes and geographical spaces in Italy. As shown, such a translation strategy clearly aims at domesticating texts that in their original version are very much based on local stereotypes and humor (Jewish/ New Yorker for *The Nanny* and small-town-American for *The Simpsons*) by shifting the humor and satire to a parallel set of local and regional stereotypes (northern vs. southern Italy).

Following the same logic of "narrative familiarity," *The Sopranos* represents the type of show that, because of the ethnic background of its original characters (Italian American), would seem a natural fit for export to a country like Italy. Besides the obvious national connection, some of the most evident dynamics and idiosyncrasies of the protagonists, from the central role of the family to the importance of food, resonate well in relation to Italian culture and customs. Thus, *The Sopranos* provides an especially useful case study of cross-cultural representation between American and Italian television.

The series is interesting even before a comparison of the two versions. First, for its overall plot and its main character: it is a mob story with a psychotic, violent, sexist, vulgar protagonist who has occasional existential crises (which allow for high levels of audience identification). Second: *The Sopranos* (which premiered in the United States in January 1999) has been almost unanimously considered one of the best television programs of the last ten years, the signature product of HBO's cinematic style and big-budget brand. Third: the series has become, in the United States at least, a real phenomenon of popular culture, and has influenced viewers' clothing, food, travel destinations, and so on.

The praise, however, has not been undisputed. Strongly based on ethnic stereotypes, *The Sopranos* has enraged Italian American associations throughout the United States, which complain about the never-ending representations of Italian Americans as gangsters. In addition, the series has also been harshly criticized for its blatant racism against all people of color, especially blacks and Latinos, who are portrayed almost exclusively as drug dealers (in opposition to Italian American mobsters, who are shown as never involving drugs in their criminal activities). Once again, *The Sopranos* offers evidence of American television as highly based on conventional representations of ethnic characters who need to be recontextualized once the series is exported abroad.

The particular questions this chapter poses about the importation and translation of *The Sopranos* in Italy are: (1) How does Italian television translate and adapt foreign stereotypes and irony about an Italian-related ethnic group that is portrayed in a particularly negative light?; (2) How do Italian audiences, accustomed to more conservative and reassuring narratives made for family viewing, respond to a TV series whose content and visuals are particularly violent and clearly aimed at adult viewers?; and (3) How does Italian television deal with the subject of the Mafia, negotiating U.S. fictional narratives with the national reality of the Mafia in the Italian news?

The Sopranos is also particularly significant when it is compared to an earlier Italian TV series, *La Piovra* (The Octopus [referring to the Mafia], 1984–1999), the most successful national TV series to date, which deals explicitly with the Mafia, but in a much different (and less romanticized) light. Created at first as a miniseries of six episodes and later developed for more than a decade into a longer series, *La Piovra* has proven that the subject of the Mafia on Italian television is both highly marketable and highly problematic. *La Piovra* will be discussed in more depth below. It is useful to point out here, however, that the show preceded the importation of *The Sopranos* in Italy, and one could argue that it "prepared" Italian audiences for a television series about the Mafia. Given its adult content, *I Soprano* (the Italian title) was never aimed at a large audience in Italy. Consequently, the series became, from the very beginning, a cult phenomenon (rather than a widespread trend of popular culture), relegated to a midnight-hour programming schedule. It was thus a failure as a major commercial success. While the violence, nudity, and language of the show undoubtedly have a lot to do with the network's decision to air *The Sopranos* in a late-night slot, it is still surprising that the popularity of the series in the United States and certain of its "familiar" themes have not been exploited to market *I Soprano* as a successful prime-time program. After all, if *The Nanny* and *The Simpsons* have been domesticated to the point of changing some of the characters' ethnicity and accents to match Italian sensibilities, one could legitimately suppose that a series such as *The Sopranos* should be a major hit for Italian audiences because of its built-in "familiarity," let alone its high production values.

I argue that *The Sopranos* represents for Italian television and Italian audiences a problematic product both familiar and foreign, for several reasons connected to its themes, its characteristics at the level of production, the decisions made about programming, its reception, and its connections to national sentiments. This chapter explores the negotiations at play when an imported show gets "too close to home" or, at least, too close to uncomfortable national problems. The translation of *The Sopranos*, therefore, constantly balances the familiar and the unfamiliar, bringing the text home when domestication is needed, or making the text foreign when it becomes too controversial.

The following sections examine these elements, compare *The Sopranos* with Italian productions about the Mafia, and analyze the generic, structural, linguistic, and cultural factors involved in such a balance between the familiar and the foreign once the show is translated into Italian.

Domesticating the Foreign . . . and Vice Versa: Selling Global Television

In Chapter 2 I introduced and discussed one of the key aspects of translation theory, which involves the choice, made by all translators, between a *domesticating* method that brings the author back home, and a *foreignizing* method that sends the reader abroad.[1] All translations, indeed, have to negotiate the gap between different readers by reestablishing linguistic and cultural references that might get lost in the transfer. As Milly Buonanno has convincingly discussed (see Chapter 2), the export and import of television is strongly based on the same dynamics of domestication and foreignization, and the efforts toward *making familiar* or *making strange* an imported text for domestic audiences (a process she defines as "the paradigm of indigenization") can represent a successful strategy both for cognitive and narrative purposes.[2]

The question that this chapter intends to answer is how this balance between the familiar and the unfamiliar is at play in the translation of *The Sopranos* in Italy. As mentioned above, I argue that through both processes of domestication and foreignization, the translation of *The Sopranos* for Italian audiences "plays" with cultural specificity, recontextualizing the original text, which is, already in itself, very much balanced between the familiar and the unfamiliar.

Before moving to the actual analysis of *The Sopranos* in Italy, it is useful to clarify this last point about the general familiarity and unfamiliarity of the series. Two articles examining the reception of *The Sopranos* in Britain and Canada apply the domestication/foreignization theory to the U.S. series quite directly. In this case, the research focuses on audience reception instead of translation. The text examined is the English version broadcast in Britain and Canada, so talking about actual translation is inappropriate. Nonetheless, both authors—Joanne Lacey and Dawn Johnston, respectively—stress the idea of national and cultural transfer of the series to two countries whose common denominator with the United States is language, but the cognitive experience of viewing is very much culturally distinct. Lacey interviews a range of British male viewers and reports data collected on the perceived "nationality" of the show:

For the interviewees the Americaness [*sic*] of the show is significant. This Americaness is, of course, a particular version of Italian Americaness that may represent as much of a fantasy, mythology, and stereotype to American audiences as it does to British. From my research it is apparent that America operates in *The Sopranos* as a landscape of both the *foreign* and the *familiar*. (emphasis added)[3]

Similarly, Johnston analyzes comments sent by Canadian viewers to the network that broadcast *The Sopranos* (CTV) and examines their perception of the show in its connection, or lack thereof, to Canadian-ness:

"As distinctly un-Canadian as this ground-breaking show may be in terms of its aesthetics, writing, subject, and spirit, it draws Canadian viewers in a ferocious and tenacious way. Perhaps there is some point of *familiarity* or connection for Canadian viewers in the smart writing or convincing portrayal of family in *The Sopranos,* or perhaps it is precisely the *lack of familiarity* that tunes many of us in and keeps us watching" [emphasis added].[4]

The Sopranos, then, seems to be very much constructed around certain myths and stereotypes that engage viewers while repulsing them at the same time. Of course, the high production values and strong scripts, on the one hand, and the violence, the nudity, and the coarse language, on the other, have a lot to do with this precarious balance in the reception experience of *The Sopranos.* However, as Lacey and Johnston demonstrate for Britain and Canada (and as I aim to do for Italy), the audiences' engagement/alienation goes beyond the series's aesthetic values or its problematic content. Tony Soprano is the next-door neighbor, yet a Mafia boss; he is very much a product of the twentieth-century United States, yet he is portrayed as an ethnic "Other"; he fights Italian American stereotypes, yet reconfirms them all. Tony Soprano's character, both as a Mafia boss and as an "American," is constructed around an extremely strong representation of *identity:* national, ethnic, social, historical, economic, geographical, linguistic, sexual, generic, criminal, familial, religious, moral, culinary, and so on. As David Chase, the series's creator explains, "We love mobsters because they look like they have strong identities and the rest of us don't."[5] My interest, then, lies in the analysis of how such strong identities travel across cultures and nations when television programs are exported/imported and consequently translated and adapted.

The Sopranos in Italy: Familiarity and Domestication

General/Global Factors

Before dealing with specific national factors in *The Sopranos* that might appeal to or, at least, simply "look and sound familiar" to Italian audiences, it is worth paying some attention to the more general, global factors that arguably make the series popular and "familiar" worldwide. In particular, two elements related to show's generic formula explain the interest and praise *The Sopranos* has received at home as well as abroad:

the narrative of the crime/gangster drama and the seriality of the family melodrama/prime-time soap. The former element, the gangster saga, grounds its roots in a long literary and cinematic tradition of mob representations, most specifically Italian American, that have characterized Hollywood since its early days and have almost always been generally successful.

Among the most intriguing storytelling sagas, mob narratives still capture the collective imaginary of viewers and readers around the world by mixing literary and cinematic genres with actual, ongoing criminal activities. Real-life mob affairs, in fact, have been nourishing Mafia narratives for decades, while gangster movies have developed, in return, plots and rhetorical tools to heighten the impact of such news events. The *New York Times* report of Michael "Mikey Scars" DiLeonardo's hearings in court, held in New York City in February 2006, is quite illuminating in this respect. Recounting his original and official oath to organized crime, Mr. DiLeonardo explained how:

he was taken to a room and seated at a long table next to Sammy Gravano, a consigliere in the family who himself would one day turn into a government witness. "We've been watching you," Mr. Gravano told him. "This is not a club. This is a secret society. There is one way into this society, the way you come in today, and one way out—on a slab." Mr. Gravano pricked Mr. DiLeonardo's trigger finger, squeezed the blood onto a crumpled picture of a saint and set the paper on fire in Mr. DiLeonardo's cupped palms. "If I betray the oath of omertà, may my soul burn in hell like this saint."[6]

As if directly taken from *The Godfather* script, the secret hierarchical organization of the "family," the sinister rituals of the oath of omertà and loyalty, and the not-so-subtle life-threatening repercussions (should such an oath be broken) have filled the headlines of major newspapers around the globe. Italian American mob myths and jargon to this day provide the news media with the necessary dramatic language constructed around the precarious balance between fascination with "gangster" crime and repulsion for it as antisocial and evil.

As the above *New York Times* article tries to demonstrate, the Mafia seems to be going through a profound crisis even among its historic leaders, who, like DiLeonardo, are willing to collaborate with the judicial system. To make things worse, less than two months after these mob hearings in New York, Giuseppe Pisanu, then Italian minister for internal affairs, announced with triumph the arrest of Mafia *capo dei capi* (boss of the bosses) Bernardo "The Tractor" Provenzano, on the run for no less than forty-three years, captured only a few miles away from the world-famous (thanks to *The Godfather* saga) town of Corleone. If this erosion of mob loyalty and power might correctly explain the ultimate destiny of present racketeering operations, such a vision of closure is far from being true for the discourses surrounding the Mafia in mass communication. From Sicily, where the Mafia legend began, to the United States, where mobster characters turned into film stars and mob narratives developed popular fascination with dons and clans, the Mafia myths have been and are continuously reinvented, and on most occasions very successfully.

The Sopranos, in fact, is nothing but the latest adaptation of the genre, a serial for cable television, filled with cinematic visual techniques and narrative references, that has dominated television ratings, awards, and academic discussions. In this sense, then, the series represents only one further step within a very winning and marketable formula, and its success in the United States and abroad is not surprising.

First and foremost, of course, are endless and precise references to *The Godfather* (the emphasis on the family, the depiction of U.S. capitalism, etc.), while the narrative structure of the series recalls that of previous TV crime dramas such as *The Untouchables*. Within this clear gangster framework, however, Horace Newcomb argues that *The Sopranos* is based as well on universal generic conventions. In particular, Newcomb contends, three main factors make *The Sopranos* generically closer to melodramatic prime-time soap opera than to crime drama: (1) a more complex portrayal of the characters; 2) the overall decay of society, for which crime is but one of the factors responsible; and (3) the fact that the "exploration of all these states and motivations occurs in a context best described as 'familial.'"[7] The complicated plots among the "family" members (related either through actual blood lineage or solemn oath ceremonies) evoke the grandiose American prime-time soaps of the 1980s and 1990s, from *Dynasty* to *Falcon Crest* to *The Bold and the Beautiful*. Newcomb, in fact, highlights the similarities between the HBO series and *Dallas*, arguing how "the primary significance of the relationship between *The Sopranos* and *Dallas* is not the villainous central character" (Tony and J. R., respectively), but the very narrative structure of both programs, heavily based on the conventions of family melodrama.[8] Newcomb clarifies this correspondence between *The Sopranos* and *Dallas:*

Any particular alteration in relational connections—an affair, a divorce, a child planned, unplanned, unknown—ripples through pairs and triads of human binding ties, shifting power relations, accumulated knowledge, and emotional response. Clearly, the introduction, withholding, and circulation of information in *The Sopranos* is fraught with narrative possibility.[9]

One such example of "narrative possibility" comes from the sixth season of *The Sopranos* (although the entire series is based on similar relations and structures): in "Johnny Cakes," Tony is approached by an attractive real estate agent, Julianna Skiff, who offers to buy the nearby poultry store for the Jamba Juice franchise. Immediately attracted by her, Tony ends up selling the store, nonetheless asking for a better price than offered. Shortly after inviting himself to her house to sign the deal, Tony kisses Julianna and seduces her, but the image of his wife, Carmela, helping him get dressed before leaving home stops him from "going all the way." This event has two consequences: first of all, Tony recounts the episode to Dr. Melfi, his psychiatrist, to be reassured that his sexual drive will come back eventually; second, since Tony "renounced" hitting on Julianna the first time, the road is open for Tony's cousin Christopher to approach Juliana at an AA meeting. Julianna and Christopher begin a prolonged love affair, although Christopher is engaged to his pregnant girlfriend and marries her shortly thereafter. As in the best tradition of soap melodrama, one single event causes several characters to become involved, on different levels, in its consequences and ramifications: Tony, Julianna, Christopher, his girlfriend (later his wife) Kelli, Carmela, and Dr. Melfi.

Thus, referring back to Milly Buonanno's comments about the cognitive and narrative tools offered to the audiences when a story is constructed in familiar (and familial) patterns, I argue that in terms of genre analysis, the gangster tradition facilitates the "cognitive decoding" of *The Sopranos,* while the family melodrama tradition nurtures the "narrative consumption" of it. Newcomb is once again insightful in clarifying this aspect of the series:

As an "informational" source for media fictions related to the "Mafia," *The Godfather* films clearly instruct viewers regarding the world of *The Sopranos.* We know about the organizational hierarchies. We are familiar with some terminology. We know about degrees of initiation and participation. Most significantly, with regard to the work of *The Sopranos* as family melodrama, we know about degrees of status and rank. There is, finally, no way to compare the roles of Michael Corleone and Tony Soprano in terms of their relative positions within "this thing of ours." Yet, emotionally and psychologically, and hence narratively, both remain central to our understanding of what this fictional world is about and how it seems to relate to the worlds of lived experiences. Tony's connection to "our" world is much more identifiable. Even if *The Godfather* is all about "family," *The Sopranos* are far more "familiar."[10]

One of the most significant factors that further increases the general "narrative familiarity" of *The Sopranos* is its location in suburbia. A traditional arena for urban settings and urban plots, in *The Sopranos* the gangster genre takes a twist toward the outskirts of the city, to the point in which it is repeatedly clarified that Tony's jurisdiction is limited to New Jersey while Carmine Lupertazzi and Johnny "Sack" Sacramoni (Tony's actual counterpart) have control over New York, including New York City. In "Employee of the Month" from the third season, Tony gets upset at Johnny Sack because he bought a house and moved to New Jersey, informing Tony only after making the decision. Later on in the series ("Moe n' Joe" from Season 6), however, Tony convinces Johnny Sack, now in jail, to sell his New Jersey house to Tony's sister Janice. This action allows Tony to symbolically regain control over his jurisdiction by geographically (and strategically) removing a member of the rival clan outside New Jersey. In other words, Johnny Sack is reconfirmed as the New York–based urban capo, while Tony is the familial/suburban boss in New Jersey. As Dawn Lacey contends, "contextualizing the action of Tony's world in an (at times) suffocating space," and constructing his character according to specific geographical suburban coordinates and local vernacular manifestations, "bring Tony closer to the audience."[11] While Lacey does not specify whether she is referring to British or American audiences, the question that interests me and drives my research is, precisely, *which specific national audiences actually get closer to Tony and his world/identity, and how is this proximity recreated or displaced when the series travels abroad?*

Specific/National Factors

As Lacey points out, one of the main characteristics of *The Sopranos* is its New Jersey Italian American vernacular, enriched with mob slang and linguistic codes or, as *New York Times* columnist William Safire put it, "a lexicon that is loosely based on Italian words, a little real Mafia slang and a smattering of lingo remembered or made up for the show by former residents of a blue-collar neighborhood in East Boston."[12] The writers of the series borrow words from that neighborhood to create a unique linguistic blend that identifies Tony and his gang not only geographically, but also ethnically and socially. Using a metaphor taken from one of the purest expressions of mobspeak, in fact, Safire defines the language in *The Sopranos* as "coming heavy," meaning it is loaded with strong social and cultural significance.[13]

The first question to pose, then, is how this very distinct, "heavy" verbal characteristic transfers to different languages and different cultures when it is exported and translated abroad. The Italian translators and writers had, in this instance, a fairly easy task, since Tony often specifies his own origin from Italy, in particular from the city of Avellino, close to Naples. Despite the pressures that Italian film and television distributors generally put on directors of dubbing to avoid the use of regional accents and dialects, in this case the writers had a clear "excuse" to dub Tony Soprano with a Neapolitan accent, since the original text "locates" him very specifically in that area. Thus, while Tony's voice in the Italian version speaks a general Italian, several words are from the Neapolitan dialect or accent, especially when Tony is upset or in an argument. Like Tony, many other characters are defined by similar linguistic characteristics, in particular his underbosses and the members of his or other clans. The use of the mob jargon mixed with expressions from the dialect in the U.S. version, as much as the use of stronger regional accents in the Italian version, represent a narrative strategy that highlights the sense of "belonging" to the secret criminal organization as well as to a world that is increasingly changing. It is not a coincidence that the younger generations in the series (Tony's daughter, Meadow, and son. A. J., for example) do not speak the jargon or have accented voices, while Livia Soprano, Tony's mother, and Uncle Junior speak, in the dubbed version, with a particularly strong Neapolitan accent.

The use of Italian accents and dialects (which supposedly corresponds to the use of the New Jersey Italian American jargon) recreates a specific geographical communalization within Italian borders, but it also divides the characters along generational lines, a gap that in Italy is felt precisely through the use of different linguistic expressions. As a result, such a strategy facilitates the reconstitution and recognition of certain *types* and *stereotypes* within Italian borders. More specific, director of dubbing Daniela Nobili contends that "this stereotype [the Italian American mobster] is a stereotype here [in Italy] as well. The villain, boorish, yokel, arrogant, powerful mobster . . . then it wasn't that difficult."[14] Certainly, in Italy translating and adapting an "Italian" with the idiosyncrasies and modes of Italian people is not too hard.

What was harder, according to Nobili, was the transcription of those words that in the original English version are taken from the dialect of some Italian American ancestors and rearranged into a mix of Neapolitan-Sicilian-New Yorker lexicon (e.g., words such as *goomah, skeevy, agita, manudge*). Again, in Italy the use of the dialect or strong regional accents is usually associated (on television, especially) with lower-class and less educated characters. What was fundamental, therefore, was to reestablish a type of not completely correct language that was very fast and full of fragmented sentences, and to recreate some sort of vulgarity and "lack of culture." Tony, in fact, often laments his lack of higher education and regrets having to drop out of college because "Grandma and Grandpa didn't stress college" and he "got into little troubles when he was a kid."[15] The use of accents and dialects was unavoidable in this case, because it establishes hierarchies and differences among characters, and it situates such characters within a specific geography, age, class status, education, and mentality.

There is something further to say about the southern Italian accents used to identify characters as specific kinds of Italian Americans and as mobsters. The inflections from Naples or Sicily, given to the actors through the use of dubbing, are a somewhat constructed version of the original accents spoken in those areas. It is very common for Italian American characters in dubbed films to have Roman actors erase their original pronunciation and speak with a southern Italian accent, which, to native Italian speakers, sounds ultimately artificial. Such a practice, far from being a foreignizing translation strategy that confuses the audience, represents, on the contrary, a widely used convention that informs the viewers about the Italian American origin of the characters. Director of dubbing Gianni Galassi, involved in the adaptation of *The Sopranos* in Italy, explains:

> To the Italian viewer that accent is a cue that the character is not Italian at all, but Italian American. When an Italian hears a character speaking ordinary street Italian on TV, that means he is an American. It's a kind of code developed from all the American movies and TV shows we import. Real Italians on television speak more correctly. *Fake television Ital-*

ian is a language we all understand, but that almost none of us speak in real life [emphasis added].[16]

This tendency toward the use of "correct" Italian cannot be generalized to every single television show produced nationally, since, as mentioned in Chapter 1, there are instances of strongly regionalized voices in contemporary programs (one striking example being the reformatted version of *Deal or No Deal*, where the twenty monetary prizes are presented by twenty members of the audience, each one coming from one of the twenty regions in Italy). It is true, however, that in television fiction the common preference is to erase the regional inflections of the actors and have them speak "proper" Italian (at least from the point of view of TV executives and distributors). Fifty years after the first TV programs broadcast in Italy, it seems that television fiction still maintains the task of "educating" Italians about their own language by providing a bland dialogue that sounds, in the end, as "artificial" as the prefabricated regional accents used in dubbing. Constructed or not, however, these inflections establish stereotypical portrayals of characters that are decoded through familiar cognitive and viewing patterns. What is especially problematic, however, as seen in the unbalanced distribution of accents among characters in *The Simpsons*,[17] is that such linguistic stereotypes almost always include a negative or satiric representation of characters from the southern regions of Italy, which corresponds to the two-fold imagined idea of the South as either the cradle of organized crime or the rural and picturesque "Other." Drawing a comparison, then, one could argue that the negative characterization of Italian Americans portrayed as mobsters in the United States directly corresponds to the Italian representation of criminals from the South in Italy.

It is worth considering not only the changes transposed from Italian American slang to Neapolitan dialect, but also the specific changes made to the ultimate cultural significance of some dialogue. "Employee of the Month" again provides an illuminating example of some of the specific "cultural" changes made to the dialogue through its translation/adaptation in Italy. Tony and his driver, Furio Giunta, meet Ralph Cifaretto, one of Tony's business associates. While Tony and Ralph are Italian Americans, Furio is originally from Naples and has moved to New Jersey to work for the Soprano family, after impressing Tony when he was on a business trip to Naples. As soon as Tony and Furio get out of the car, Ralph salutes them with a joke and has a conversation with Furio:

Ralphie: How many Neapolitans does it take to screw in a light bulb? There's only candles in Naples right now, the cardinals of the church control that racket.
Furio: That's a good one!
Ralphie: You like it? You can have it! Use it on your paisans.
Furio: We don't have those bulb jokes, they don't translate.

The last sentence of the dialogue is particularly interesting, first of all because it self-referentially plays with the idea of cultural and linguistic translation. Second, the sentence becomes somewhat problematic for Italian translators, because *logically* it would not make sense for Furio to claim that a joke cannot be transposed into Italian when all the characters in the dialogue are indeed speaking Italian already. Thus, the Italian version (provided below together with a literal translation) changes the last sentence of the dialogue, turning the reference to the "un-translatability" of the joke into a cultural and national joke about the Vatican and the Catholic Church:

Italian version
Ralphie: Quanti napoletani ci vogliono per svitare una lampadina? Nessuno, ci sono solo candele a Napoli, perche' un cardinale controlla il racket.
Furio: Questa e' buona!
Ralphie: Se ti piace raccontala ai tuoi paesani.
Furio: No, non funziona in Italia, con la Chiesa non si scherza.

Literal translation
Ralphie: How many Neapolitans does it take to screw in a light bulb? No one, there are only candles in Naples, because a cardinal controls that racket.
Furio: That's a good one!
Ralphie: If you like it, tell it to your paisanos.
Furio: No, it doesn't work in Italy, you can't mess with the church.

Italian audiences can now understand the dialogue, which works fairly well in recreating the humor of the original text, transposing a linguistic joke into a cultural and national one. The joke lies in the idea that since the Vatican and the Catholic Church are omnipresent in Italian life and often propose and *impose* certain conservative behavioral standards, common are the instances in which people actually "mess with them" and disapprove, as opposed to what Furio ironically claims.

These efforts toward linguistic domestication, together with Tony's reference to Avellino and Naples (as well as an actual episode shot in Naples during Tony's business trip to Italy) and the use of accents and dialect from the southern Italian region of Campania, place *The Sopranos* in very precise spots within Italian culture and geography. One major complaint the series received in Italy, in fact, was from Antonio Di Nunno, the mayor of Avellino who, when interviewed by the *New York Times* about his opinion of a crime drama referring to his city, answered, "I don't know why they had to pick us. We're not Corleone."[18] Di Nunno symbolizes in this statement the discourse of the Mafia as portrayed in the media: the constant presence of organized crime in the news and the fostering of the myth by literary and cinematic fiction. Corleone, in fact, a small hill town fifty-six kilometers away from Palermo (Sicily), was put on the map by Mario Puzo and Francis Ford Coppola in *The Godfather* saga. Its symbolic status has grown through the years as a place where the line between myth and real crime blurs, and it was recently "rediscovered" as a bona fide Mafia location after the arrest there of boss of the bosses Bernardo "The Tractor" Provenzano on April 11, 2006.

The topic of the Mafia, then, is an additional factor, which together with the vernacular elements and the specific changes to the text allows *The Sopranos* to be perceived in Italy within a familiar framework. Notwithstanding the critiques of a number of communication scholars in Italy who argue that the subject of the Mafia is inadequately discussed on Italian television, especially in its tight relation with politics, the Mafia is omnipresent in Italian news and fiction, with more or less sensational headlines, the arrest of Provenzano being one of the major ones in the last decade. This perseverance is indeed what frustrates critical discussions about the Mafia in Italy, discussions that accuse television of ignoring the real issues at stake while focusing on fictional narratives.[19] Communication scholar Giovanni Bechelloni describes the Mafia as a "giant in the collective imaginary of half the world" and considers it "the best known Italian product in the world."[20] However, he adds:

> Mafia is also, in recent years, a real obsession for Italians. The Mafia is the rock against which the "Italian dream" crashed, the dream which had nourished the collective imaginary since the "miracle" years at the end of the 1950s, and in the heart of the tragic years of terrorism in the

1970s and in the enthusiasm of the 1980s. Mafia represents today [1995] the empire of evil, the incarnation of everything negative, the occultism that lies behind any important actions related to money, power, financing, politics, success, and wealth. The melancholic 1990s are, at first, characterized by the omnipresence of the Mafia.[21]

In the news and in fictional narrative, both a fascinating myth and a painful memory, the Mafia is phenomenally marketable in Italy thanks to the American gangster tradition, but also thanks to national television productions that have dominated ratings on Italian television in the 1980s and the 1990s. As mentioned previously, the most significant example of this trend is the series *La Piovra,* produced by RAI and released initially as a miniseries of six episodes in March 1984. The main character, Corrado Cattani, chief of police, fights against crime in Sicily in a Mafia story that draws its plot from mob literature as much as from Mafia news. The series, considered a genuine popular phenomenon and a symbol of Italian national identity, was so successful that it continued for ten seasons over fifteen years (the tenth season was released in 1999). Very similarly to *The Sopranos, La Piovra* mixed Mafia narrative traditions with contemporary news and played with the balance between repulsion and fascination with mobsters. Beyond Italian television, *La Piovra* was also successful internationally, becoming the first example, in Italy, of exportable global television based on strictly national stories. The global dimension of *La Piovra* is demonstrated by the fact that the series was translated and exported to countries all over Europe, on a scale that was certainly a novelty at the time and is still unsurpassed today. The series, however, was also "global" for another significant reason. The first season, in particular, was so popular that it managed to compete directly with the major American series of the time, *Dallas.* Interestingly enough, *La Piovra* was defined as "the Italian response to *Dallas*"[22] and analyzed generically as "social melodrama" beyond its gangster components (much as Newcomb has demonstrated the relation of *The Sopranos* to "family melodrama").

It seems, then, that a crime drama that mixes mobster narrative with melodramatic plots is nothing new for Italian audiences, and that a market for *The Sopranos* would be easy to find just by "recycling" the original audience of *La Piovra. The Sopranos,* however, broadcast by Mediaset on Canale 5 and then moved to cable on demand, has been relegated to a midnight-hour schedule since its first season, and has failed to become the commercial success or popular cultural phenomenon it was in the United States. What is new, and foreign perhaps, is the explicit way certain themes are portrayed in *The Sopranos,* specifically the violent and highly sexual visuals to which Italian audiences are not accustomed, especially on prime time. The "length" of the series (six seasons broadcast between 1999 and 2007) also represents a foreign phenomenon for Italian television, since most prime-time national fiction does not usually exceed six episodes total.

The following section explores these "unfamiliar" factors and examines some of the decisions made about the show's scheduling and translation, as well as the reasons why the series became a cult, niche program from the very beginning. I will also look at those cultural elements in *The Sopranos* that might be problematic in Italy precisely because they "hit too close to home," and therefore need to be made more foreign. The Mafia slaughters of judges Giovanni Falcone (May 1992) and Paolo Borsellino (July 1992), both of whom died in the attacks together with the police officers escorting them, still seem fresh in the memory of the Italian people. The arrest of Bernardo Provenzano is another example. In that case, while Italian television portrayed the boss's daily routines as a fugitive, Italians, and especially Sicilians, poured into the streets celebrating his capture and manifesting their hatred of organized crime. Thus, the dichotomy between the "soft" media coverage of the Mafia in Italy and the strong sensibility of the citizens against what is perceived to be a painful national "cancer," certainly explains, or at least puts in context, some of the decisions made about the importation of *The Sopranos* in Italy.

The Sopranos in Italy: Foreignization and Displacement

Structural Elements and Programming

I will focus first on the structural elements at the level of production in order to analyze what factors in *The Sopranos* might be perceived as "foreign" by Italian audiences. As introduced above, long seriality on prime time is unusual in Italy since most nationally produced miniseries develop through two to six episodes (at most eight, in rare cases). The most popular form of television fiction for prime time is the *sceneggiato* (miniseries), a narrative representation of subject matter that can be both completely fictional or, as it often happens, based on historical or literary figures and events. Besides those that are nationally produced, some *sceneggiati* are coproduced by Italy and other European countries, and there are also a few cases of non-European productions. The first example of *sceneggiato* (produced by RAI) dates back to 1954: *Il dottor Antonio,* based on a novel by Giovanni Ruffini dealing with the Italian risorgimento in the nineteenth century. Some other examples of *sceneggiati* include: *Mosé* (1974) and *Gesú di Nazareth* (1977), both British-Italian coproductions; and *Marco Polo* (an eight-episode mini-series, broadcast in 1982 on RAI and coproduced by Italy and the United States, with a high-quality international cast including Anne Bancroft, Burt Lancaster, John Gielgud, and Leonard Nimoy).[23] Two of the latest examples of successful *sceneggiati* are *Giovanni Paolo II* (Pope John Paul II), produced by CBS in 2005 and broadcast on RAI 1, and *Papa Luciani: Il sorriso di Dio* (Pope Luciani: The smile of God), produced by RAI in October 2006 and based on the life of Pope John Paul I. While some *sceneggiati* are coproduced or completely foreign, and there are examples of shows not necessarily related to purely nationalistic themes, most miniseries broadcast in Italy on prime time are based on Italian literary classics, historical events, religious figures, or at least on themes reflecting some sort of national sensibility, often geared toward the family. Hence, the *sceneggiato* is very much a "national" product both in terms of structure (short seriality) and in terms of narrative content. The 2002 annual report by Eurofiction (the most significant research project monitoring television fiction in Europe) shows how both public and private television in Italy are recently investing more consistently in longer series, which seem fairly profitable for the networks. However, the report also shows how both RAI and Mediaset still focus primarily on the production of miniseries, to which they dedicate "half of their titles, major editorial attention, and the most significant investments."[24] Further, as Buonanno contends, in terms of branding, miniseries give networks their specific identity, what broadcasters in Italy call "the enlightenment of the network," by reconciling ratings and quality, popularity and culture, which often seem to lie on opposite poles.[25]

There is, in fact, some distrust and arrogance (among both Italian audiences and critics) toward long serials, which are "seen as something *foreign* to 'our' culture, and often associated with the *cheap* and intrusive products of the colonizing American television culture."[26] Buonanno's discussions about the narrative and cognitive balance between the familiar and unfamiliar on Italian television, in fact, goes beyond the actual stories told in fiction, to include factors regarding flow and programming, as well as overall production structures. In other words, familiarity with a show depends on several factors that the audiences might find recognizable according to their cultural environment and also according to what they have been accustomed to watching over the years. These factors include, first of all, the actors and characters in the show, the dialogue and language they speak, and the overall story. The perceived familiarity with any given program, however, also includes: the narrative structure of the story (i.e., whether the story exhibits closure and how fast it gets to such closure); the schedule of programming (daytime, prime time, late night), which usually depends on the show's narrative structure; its targeted audience, and the money invested in it; and the overall aesthetics (programs that make use of sophisticated references to film style are more likely to be viewed as unfamiliar for a generic television audience).

For all the elements just mentioned, then, *The Sopranos* is simply the kind of show that is hard (if not impossible) to watch on Italian television any time before 11:00 p.m. or even later, despite the popularity of the series in the United States, the global appeal of crime stories, the high production values, and the strong scripts. *The Sopranos* presents, indeed, several major problems for broadcasters in Italy. I have already discussed the difficulties related to long seriality on prime time. In addition, Italian networks (especially the public network, RAI) give substantial priority to domestic productions over international imports for their prime-time slots.[27] According to broadcast logics, then, *The Sopranos* might represent a bad choice for prime-time scheduling simply because it is (literally) "foreign." Further, the general attitude of Italian network executives is to opt for reassuring and not-too-complicated plots, and hence for a type of program anchored in tradition, both in terms of narrative and in terms of aesthetics, specifically because programming is "conceived for a familial and generic audience."[28] Generally speaking, it is clear that *The Sopranos* is not a series conceived for a general public, but rather for an adult and educated audience. Even in the United States, the series was never envisioned for mainstream broadcasting; indeed, it was rejected by Fox for basic cable television and ended up being produced by HBO for pay cable. It was only in 2005 that *The Sopranos* was finally sold for syndication to the basic-cable network A&E, at the record rate of $2.5 million per episode (a total of about $195 million for the entire series) and began airing in an edited version in January 2007.[29]

Director of dubbing Daniela Nobili explains how Mediaset bought the series in 2001 because it was undoubtedly popular on an international scale, and also to take it away from RAI (although, according to

Nobili, the rival network would have never bought it anyway because it was too different from its usual programs).[30] Once Mediaset owned the rights to the series they had to dub it, but instead of opting for a linguistically and visually censored version to broadcast on prime time (the option A&E chose in the United States, to maximize profits and attract a larger audience), Mediaset decided on an "uncensored"[31] version to broadcast, at first on its chief channel, Canale 5, at 11:00 p.m. Buonanno reports that the decision to air the series around midnight generated some protests among both critics and viewers, who complained that such an innovative program deserved a better time slot.[32] Another complaint from the few and faithful fans of *The Sopranos* in Italy regarded the extreme randomness in the programming of the series; depending on the duration of the shows scheduled right before *The Sopranos*, the series would air earlier or later than the established time with no previous notice to viewers. As Nobili ambiguously points out, such an inexplicable Mediaset "boycott" against a series that was the "hottest" show on TV as a whole does not seem to be completely random. The following section, then, raises a few more explanations, beyond the structural factors, that might have caused such a "cold" reaction to *The Sopranos* in Italy.

Mafia: This Thing of Ours

I have already discussed the success that *La Piovra* (the only national fiction dealing specifically with the Mafia) had in Italy, as well as the general familiarity of crime dramas and melodramatic plots on Italian television. A few more generic factors, however, deserve further analysis. The fascination with crime shows among Italian audiences does not exclusively depend on the consumption of foreign TV series; it is also confirmed by a recurrent preference for national productions that deal with crime and justice. In this case I am not referring specifically to the gangster genre; I include series and shows that might fall under the more general umbrella of crime drama. In this regard, a few examples of recent successful Italian series and miniseries (beyond *La Piovra*) are: *Il maresciallo Rocca* (five seasons produced between 1996 and 2005 by RAI); *Il commissario Montalbano* (produced between 1999 and 2005 by RAI; fourteen episodes that each offer internal closure, although they are part of an overall story based on the novels by Sicilian writer Andrea Camilleri); *Distretto di polizia* (now airing in its tenth season on Mediaset Canale 5); and *Carabinieri* (a five-season series produced by Mediaset from 2002 to the present).

There is one striking characteristic common to all the series mentioned that characterizes Italian TV crime drama and also differentiates
them from *The Sopranos:* all the protagonists are police officers. *La Piovra* itself focuses on the figure of Chief Cattani, at first, and then on his
successor, Davide Licata, when the Mafia kills Cattani. Even though,
as Buonanno writes, there are fascinating representations of villains in
La Piovra,[33] the point of view of the story is that of the chief of police.
There are no series or miniseries produced in Italy that have criminals,
and especially mobsters, as protagonists. The portrayal of crime, then, is
much less romanticized than it is in programs imported from the United
States, because audiences always identify with detectives and police officers and never with those committing the crimes, as happens in *The
Sopranos.* In this respect, a *New York Times* article reports a conversation
between HBO executive Chris Albrecht and David Chase over "College," the fourth episode after the pilot, in which Tony, for the first time
in the series, kills a man with his bare hands:

> When he saw the episode, Chris Albrecht was appalled. "Chris said,
> you've invented one of the best leading characters in television in
> 20 years and you're going to destroy him," Mr. Chase said. "I said,
> at this point: 'This guy is a squealer. Tony is a Mob boss. If he doesn't
> kill him, you've lost more of the audience than you're going to lose if
> he does.'"[34]

Very clearly *The Sopranos* is based on the fine balance between audience
identification with Tony and repulsion from him. While such a balance
is what makes his character so rich and complex and the series so sophisticated, the fascination with criminals is problematic for Italian prime
time, filled with domestic stories about police officers, some of whom
die in the fight against crime. When it comes to the Mafia, then, its romanticized and ambivalent portrayal imported from the United States
does not always have the same appeal in Italy. Simply put, there is nothing "romantic" about the Mafia in Italy, and especially in Sicily, that
could inspire fictional stories told from the point of view of the villains.

Another difference between the representation of the Mafia in U.S.
media and Italian media concerns the social status of the criminals.
There is a clear tendency in the United States to portray mobsters as
urban criminals who have reached upper-middle-class status. Conversely,
the representation of the mafiosi in Italy always includes a rural and
peasant dimension. In film, such a representational dichotomy becomes

clear in a comparison between *The Godfather* (1972) and *Salvatore Giu-liano* (1962). The Coppola film's Don Corleone, a rich Mafia boss played by Marlon Brando, strikingly contrasts with Francesco Rosi's rural ma-fioso, who hides in the arid Sicilian countryside, does not pronounce a single line in the entire movie, and whose dead body we see carried around in a small Sicilian town without ever seeing his face. The peas-ant association with the Mafia is based on reality, and can be seen in the case of Bernardo Provenzano. After his arrest the description in the newspapers and on television mirrored the fictional rural portrayal of *Salvatore Giuliano*. The news repeated over and over how the boss was found in a farmhouse in the outskirts of Corleone, "betrayed" by brief encoded messages handwritten on small pieces of paper (*pizzini*) deliv-ered to him with his clean underwear. Tony Soprano's suburban life and upper-middle-class status, therefore, contrast sharply with the general idea about mobsters that people have in Italy. As opposed to what Lacey claims for British and American viewers, I would argue that moving the action to New Jersey and suburbia only heightens the unfamiliarity of the show for Italian audiences.

This suburban aspect is emphasized very clearly in the opening credits in which we see Tony drive home to New Jersey, leaving New York City behind, and ending up in a suburban area that, for the Italian view-ers, could be anywhere (and nowhere) in the United States. This setting doubly defamiliarizes Tony Soprano, since he is represented as neither the rural Italian mafioso nor the glamorous Italian American gangster à la Al Capone.

All of the defamiliarizing factors I have described might also explain the only form of "censorship" *The Sopranos* has undergone in the Italian translation. As Daniela Nobili reveals:

> The only change the Italian network imposed for the translation was to never pronounce the word "Mafia." Every time that some charac-ter would pronounce the word "Mafia," in the original version, we have translated and adapted with "mala," "organized crime," or bypassed the problem with no translation at all. They left the coarse language intact, but not this wound in Italian nationalism about Mafia. Not all the Ital-ians abroad are mafiosi, they might be common criminals, like there are criminals of other nationalities, but Mafia is really an Italian product, like pecorino.[35]

While there are definitely efforts made in the U.S. dialogue to "hide" Tony's relation to the Mafia, I would argue that in the original version

this strategy is a sophisticated narrative "trick," offering a form of con-
gratulatory flattery for the audience, who do not need a clear explanation about Tony's real business to know what Tony's real business is.
This subtle attitude is maintained in the Italian version, but the blatant
erasure of the actual noun *Mafia* from the dialogue (in the few instances
in which the name is actually pronounced in the original text) seems to
serve other cultural purposes.

One such elision comes from the episode "College." Tony escorts his
daughter, Meadow, on a series of visits to colleges in Maine, and in the
car Meadow asks Tony whether he is involved in criminal activities.

Original U.S. dialogue
Meadow: Are you in the Mafia?
Tony: Am I in the what?
Meadow: Whatever you want to call it, organized crime.
Tony: That's total crap, who told you that?
. . .
Meadow: Did other kids ever find fifty thousand dollars in Krugerrands
   and a forty-five automatic while they were hunting for Easter eggs?
Tony: I'm in the waste management business; everybody immediately
   assumes you're mobbed-up. It's a stereotype, and it's offensive. . . .
   There is no Mafia.

Italian version
Meadow: Tu sei della mala?
Tony: Come hai detto, scusa?
Meadow: Ma si, hai capito, il crimine organizzato.
Tony: Ma chi te l'ha detta questa stronzata?
. . .
Meadow: I figli degli altri hanno mai trovato 50,000 dollari in franchi
   svizzeri e una 45 automatica mentre cercavano i regali di natale?
Tony: Io mi occupo di raccolta dei rifiuti e tutti pensano che sono colle-
   gato con il crimine. E' uno stereotipo questo, ed e'offensivo. . . . Che
   cazzo c'entra la mala?
Literal translation
Meadow: Are you in the mala?[36]
Tony: What did you just say, sorry?
Meadow: Yes, I mean, organized crime.
Tony: Who told you this bullshit?
. . .
Meadow: Did other kids ever find fifty thousand dollars in Swiss francs

and a forty-five automatic while they were hunting for Christmas presents?[37]

Tony: I'm in waste management and everybody thinks I'm related to crime. It's a stereotype! And it's offensive. . . . What does mala have to do with it?

This episode, winner of the 1999 Emmy for outstanding writing, is considered one of the best shows in the series and is particularly loved by David Chase for the strength of its script. "College" is also the episode in which Tony's identity as a mobster is more clearly defined by having him kill a man for the first time in the show. As if this event were not enough, Tony's criminal character is further legitimized by Meadow's approval when, right after the dialogue above, he confesses that some of his money comes from illegal activities, and she praises him for "being a cool dad" and not lying to her. "College," then, is one of the few episodes in which the protagonist is directly and un-metaphorically put face-to-face with his role in organized crime. It is not a coincidence, then, that this is also one of the few episodes in which the word "Mafia" (and "mafioso") is pronounced in the actual (original) dialogue and not as simple background chatter in the TV news. It is also interesting to notice how, in the American version, Tony, although confessing some illegal operations, denies not only his connection with the Mafia but the actual existence of it ("There is no Mafia"). Technically, the Italian translation does not deny the existence of organized crime, since Tony simply states that "mala" has nothing to do with what he does. However, by completely erasing the word from the dialogue, a word that could easily be included in the new version since Mafia is an Italian word (and therefore would work perfectly for lip synchronization), the translation perpetrates the idea that the Mafia is a problematic subject for Italian television and therefore needs to be removed.

Two other examples from the episode further demonstrate Italian efforts to cancel any connection between *The Sopranos* and Italian mobsters. At a gas station, Tony sees Fabian Petrulio, once a member of the clan, who was caught selling heroin and ended up naming names to the FBI to reduce his punishment. Tony gets Fabian's license plate and immediately calls Christopher to obtain information. In the phone conversation, Tony explains how Fabian became part of a witness protection program and eventually earned his living by lecturing in universities about his old life as a "mafioso." Surprised, Christopher answers: "*Minchia!* And you saw this guy up in Maine?"

The Italian translation adapts the dialogue by having Tony say that Fabian now earns his money talking to students about his life as "an ugly, dirty, bad guy" (*quando era brutto, sporco e cattivo*) to which Christopher replies: "*Azz,* and you saw him in Maine?" (*Azz, e l'hai visto in Maine?*). In the first case the translation "simply" changes the word "mafioso" to "bad guy," reconfirming what Daniela Nobili reveals about the editorial choices imposed by Mediaset in the dubbing of the series. The second example, though, is more interesting because it is subtler. *Minchia* is Sicilian slang for male genitalia. *Azz,* short version of *cazzo,* is the corresponding word in Italian. The translation, then, maintains the vulgarity of the language, but completely erases the cultural and regional connotations embedded in the original version, since the word "minchia" is clearly associated with Sicily, and therefore with Mafia and mafiosi as well. In this case, then, the regional Sicilian word, which is used in the original U.S. version, is erased and substituted with a corresponding Italian term that eliminates any possible controversial reference to Sicily and the Mafia.

Variety helps contextualize the changes made to the dialogue in relation to specific events happening in Italy at the time. *The Sopranos* debuted in Italy in 2001 on Mediaset's Canale 5. The same year, Silvio Berlusconi, Mediaset's main shareholder, was elected prime minister, but he was still "entangled in legal suits alleging that he had ties to the Mafia."[38] While the article in *Variety* does not mention the erasure of the word "Mafia" from the Italian dialogue, by putting the importation of *The Sopranos* in Italy in the context of Berlusconi's election and ongoing mob trial, it certainly provides one of the possible (as well as disturbing) explanations for the specific form of linguistic censorship that the series has undergone in Italy.

Concluding Remarks: How Tony Is Afraid of Naples (and So Are We)

Whether such controversial editorial choices were made so as to avoid hurting viewers' national feelings, and should therefore be considered censorship, is debatable. Nobili contends that the idea behind the erasure of the word "Mafia" from the dialogue was to stop perpetrating the stereotype that all Italian Americans are mobsters. But by adding that the choice of airing *I Soprano* late at night was not completely random, she seems to imply that other elements were involved in the ultimate

decisions about the series's translation and programming. This opinion resonates well with some of the critical discussions about organized
crime and Italian media, discussions that openly criticize Italian television for ignoring in its crime fiction the real issues at stake in relation to
the Mafia and organized crime (i.e., their close relation with politics).
Quite frankly, erasing the word "Mafia" from a series such as *The Sopranos* does not seem to have any explanation other than as a form of
censorship.

Best-selling writer Roberto Saviano confirms this idea in a precise
analysis of the series. Author of *Gomorra,* Saviano offers a brutal account
of organized crime in Naples that "digs deep inside the gangsters' world,
naming names, spelling out criminal structures and their ways of working, drawing a detailed picture of a city which, in his analysis, has largely
surrendered to the criminals."[39] In his commentary about *The Sopranos,*
Saviano discusses the episode "Commendatori" ("Viaggio in Italia" in
its Italian title), in which Tony, Christopher, and Paulie travel to Naples.
Saviano sarcastically invites the mayor of Naples, Rosa Russo Iervolino,
to "watch the episode with zeal and diligence" to learn something about
the city she runs.[40] Saviano contends that by dealing with waste management, illegal urban development, and stolen cars, Tony Soprano is
actually closer to Naples (cradle of the crime organization Camorra)
than to Palermo (cradle of the Mafia). But once in Naples, the capital
of international organized crime, "the Italian-American gangsters feel
microscopic . . . amazed by the ease with which people shoot and kill in
Naples." And Naples becomes, "in the eyes of *The Sopranos,* the [true]
nucleus of power."[41] Thus, Saviano brings essential evidence to the idea
that the series indeed came too close to Italian news, and praises *The
Sopranos* for being the first fictional account that introduced the United
States (and perhaps Italy as well) to the real Naples.

A few other elements deserve further analysis. The last season, which
aired on HBO in 2007, focuses on the idea of decline, not only of the
series and Tony, first, but also a decline that involves more general and
deeper social factors. There are, for example, various references made
about the new corporate organizations and store chains, such as Star-
bucks, that are able to bypass control and protection by the local gangsters. The series plays with this concept ironically, having the mobsters
complaining about the decay of American society once everything is
controlled by corporations (as opposed to organized crime). While in
Italy globalization and corporate capitalism have certainly already entered the economic and cultural scene, it still seems that the speed of

these transformations is not as fast or visible as it is in the United States. It will be interesting, therefore, to see how the not-so-subtle critiques of global capitalism are translated, and eventually recreated, in Italy.

One more thing also needs to be said about the recent scheduling and programming of the series in Italy. Since May 2006, Mediaset has been airing *I Soprano* on demand on its pay-per-view channel, Mediaset Premium (two episodes each Thursday night starting at 10:45 p.m.), offering different rates depending on the number of episodes one buys: two euros for a single evening (two episodes), nine euros for each entire season, and thirty-nine euros for the complete six-season package.[42] Cable television and especially television on demand are fairly new phenomena in Italy, a trend that has developed more significantly only in the last few years. As the 2002 Eurofiction report shows, what slows down the diffusion of digital cable television in Italy is some sort of "cultural resistance felt by the majority of Italians who find it hard to abandon the idea that television is a *free* medium."[43] Further, the programs offered on cable television are not yet able to compete with those offered by regular television channels. Although this might sound incomprehensible for U.S. viewers used to HBO's high quality of programming, regular broadcasting in Italy offers richer and more diverse products than most countries in Europe. Thus, the appeal of narrowcasting (i.e., paid cable) is less attractive for both the audience and the TV executives who might invest in it. *The Sopranos,* then, moved to a medium, pay-per-view, which itself remains foreign to most Italians.[44]

As just examined in the chapter, even though innovative, smart, and sophisticated, *The Sopranos* presents several problems for Italian networks in terms of its narrative structure, visual style, and cultural significance. The idea of *cultural discount,* according to which a program exported abroad diminishes in value to the advertisers and the broadcasters because it is less appealing to the new audiences, might thus explain the decision to market *The Sopranos* as a niche, cult series as opposed to a general phenomenon of popular culture.[45] Certainly, the market value of *The Sopranos* is much lower for Mediaset in Italy than, for example, for A&E in the United States. After spending $2.5 million per episode, A&E certainly cannot afford to relegate the series to a late-night programming slot, or to market *The Sopranos* as a cult show. The popularity the series has gained at home and the vast domestic audience available in the United States have allowed HBO to sell *The Sopranos* in syndication at the highest price ever paid for a series's reruns in the United States.[46] However, such success and audience appeal do not necessarily travel abroad just because *The Sopranos* is generally regarded as a "great series." As seen in this chapter, negotiations are at play in terms of programming, narrative, and cultural factors once a "global" show is exported. Mediaset, ultimately lacking the security that A&E was granted by HBO's massive marketing campaign in the United States, still decided to buy the series, but has played it safe by not risking its prime-time programming. And as discussed in Chapter 1, the strategy to dedicate prime time, the most profitable and watched time slot of the day, to national productions mirrors the general approach adopted not only by Italian broadcasters, but broadcasters across the rest of Europe as well.

Translating Stereotypes: The Cultural Politics of Reformatting

The preceding chapters have demonstrated how television dubbing, one specific case of reformatting, allows for globally distributed programs to be indigenized for local audiences. More broadly, this book has argued against a commonly held interpretation of global media processes: that there is a direct relation between one country's economic supremacy in media export and its corresponding cultural domination over other nations. In fact, if it is true that the United States is a leading producer and distributor of television programs worldwide, it is also true that these shows need to be adapted, translated, and remarketed for new national audiences in each new environment where they are imported. This study has focused on linguistic issues of audiovisual translation to argue that dubbing provides a rich array of tools that allow national media industries to domesticate distributed television texts for national audiences.

Thus, instead of considering international media flows in the light of the cultural imperialist paradigm, this study has examined and validates the thesis that complex cultural and industrial negotiations are at play when individual countries import globally distributed programs. In taking this approach, and contrary to several discussions in international media studies, the emphasis shifts from the (dominant) point of view of the exporting countries, to the dynamic (and somehow resistant) point of view of the receivers—the importing countries.

Through dubbing, indigenization plays out on multiple levels. The characters' names and origin can be modified (as happens in *The Nanny* and *The Simpsons*); the characters' relations with one another can change for purposes of decency (as is the case with Sylvia and Yetta in *The Nanny*); the characters' ethnic, cultural, and religious backgrounds can be domesticated for a better understanding of the overall program (as the change from Jewish American to Italian American in *The Nanny* demonstrates); accents and regional dialects can be used in particularly effective ways to re-territorialize the characters within a new national context (as happens to many characters in *The Simpsons*); and some elements of the show can be eliminated if they are too controversial in the new context (as is the case with the erasure of the word "Mafia" in the Italian version of *The Sopranos*). These are only a few examples of how a text can be indigenized through dubbing, which can be productively considered as a form of *cultural ventriloquism* able to erase one "dominant voice" and substitute it with a new "national voice."

Further, the case studies analyzed here have demonstrated how ethnicity and language function as two fundamental elements that undergo modifications in the processes of indigenization. The three television series' use of stereotypes, narrative forms, humor, and irony are heavily based on ethnic and linguistic codes: New York/Jewish stereotypes and accents (*The Nanny*), Italian American stereotypes and jargon (*The Sopranos*), and a variety of both American and international idiosyncrasies exploited for purposes of comedy (*The Simpsons*). All three texts construct their characters according to specific regional and ethnic elements, which are transferred to the new Italian context "simply" by substituting a new dialogue. The original stereotypical connotations of these "American texts" are thus reconfigured in translation and culturally adapted for the new Italian audience according to corresponding stereotypical narratives of the nation. The transfer of these ethnic characters—and caricatures—not only provides evidence about Italian television as an industry that employs conventional myths of the nation to establish hierarchies of "Otherness," but also confirms American television as the very site of origin for such stereotypes and caricatures.

The evidence provided by the analysis of *The Nanny*, *The Simpsons*, and *The Sopranos* shows, in fact, how the domestication of TV programs is not limited to certain series that share recurrent narrative elements, but happens throughout different genres, includes products targeted to diverse audiences, and is produced for both network and cable television. The three series examined "belong" to three different kinds of popular (American) genre categorizations and modes of narration: situation comedy (*The Nanny*), animated comedy (*The Simpsons*), and gangster melodrama (*The Sopranos*). Also, the three series target different gender and age groups: adult women (*The Nanny*), adult men (*The Sopranos*), and the younger generation (*The Simpsons*). (Although *The Simpsons* in the United States appeals to and mainly targets an adult audience, in Italy the series has been clearly marketed as a media product for teenager consumption.) In sum, *Since When Is Fran Drescher Jewish?* has dealt with issues of cultural identity, language, and globalization across different genres, taking into consideration a wide range of spectators, so as to suggest a broader application for the theoretical conclusions it draws.

In addition, the three series have been produced and broadcast by different networks and cable channels in the United States: *The Nanny* was produced by Sony and aired on the CBS network from 1993 to 1999, and now is in syndication on Lifetime; *The Simpsons* was produced by Fox and Gracie Films and has aired on Fox from 1989 to the present, and is syndicated on Fox as well; and *The Sopranos* was produced by and aired on HBO pay cable from 1999 to 2007, and now is syndicated on A&E. Considering series aired on both network TV and pay cable demonstrates that ethnic stereotypes are a generally profitable marketing strategy for American television, and that forms of localization are applied in translation to the most diverse programs imported abroad, not only across genres, production values, and visual style but also across the industrial environment in which such programs are originally produced and in which they are shown. This analysis suggests that diverse tendencies in Hollywood industrial practice pass under the indigenization lens once exported abroad.

What stands out from the analysis of the three case studies is the fact that domestication is based on certain imagined narratives of the nation that presuppose the existence of imagined "televisual communities" who share certain values and beliefs. In Italy, such narratives are based on the traditional separation between North and South, are nurtured by the profound regionalism that characterizes the country and its identity, and are scrutinized under the influence of the strong censoring eye of the Catholic Church. What emerges from this scenario is that the "imagined idea of Italy," constructed in audiovisual translation and sold to the new audience, employs and exploits certain cultural stereotypes of the nation that are built on and continuously recreated on the basis of those narratives.

In particular, the South (and the dialects and accents associated with it) offers a twofold possibility for stereotypical representation: on the one hand, in the picturesque image of folkloric Italy, and on the other, in the shameful reality of organized crime. Given the imaginary and essentialist dual "nature" of the South, it can be argued that comedy in Italy has traditionally been associated with the first stereotype of the South, while drama has conventionally been constructed on the basis of the second. The series analyzed here are no exception. The translators of *The Nanny* and *The Simpsons* seem to privilege the stereotypical representation of the South as an arena for pictureque and ironic depictions of a rural, unsophisticated lifestyle. The adaptation of *The Sopranos,* however, finds fertile ground in the dramatic idea of the South as the cradle of the Mafia and organized crime.

As discussed in the book, both connotations associated with this "imagined South" end up offering the most recurrent (if not the only) "place" for Otherness represented on Italian television. The concern here is that, when forced into this limited narrative scenario, certain indigenous manifestations of diversity and "Otherness" risk being erased if they don't fit that imagined but anachronistic idea of the Italian nation. The original Jewishness of *The Nanny,* for example, is modified (and thus erased) because of the lack of familiarity Italians have with the cultural depiction of Jewish Americans; problematizing the idea of indigenization discussed in the book, this erasure somehow marks a step back toward cultural homogenization (if examined from the point of view of the original text).

This constructed idea of the nation, therefore, "dictates" what changes need to be made to series imported from foreign countries, and, as was demonstrated, such changes tend to follow two major tendencies in the practice of translation. On the one hand, translators and dialogue writers domesticate what is strange and unfamiliar to make it more appealing to the new audience. On the other, dubbing practitioners often need to foreignize and displace certain problematic elements that might hurt national feelings and therefore might alienate the new audience. This balance between *domestication* and *foreignization* lies at the core of every theory of translation that addresses the efforts made to recontextualize a text from one cultural environment to another. Audiovisual translations, therefore, are but one example of cultural transfer.

Considering, however, that audiovisual translations make international media distribution possible, it becomes clear how a truly comprehensive analysis of dubbing must apply an interdisciplinary methodology of analysis that takes into consideration both translation studies and media studies. As this research has attempted to demonstrate, in fact, such a methodological approach should consider dubbing from two main perspectives. Dubbing should be examined under the theoretical lens of translation studies as a form of cultural ventriloquism that allows the indigenization of texts. Yet the analysis of dubbing must take into consideration the efficacy of textual analysis, the findings of audience reception studies, and the industrial aspects of television practices that can only come from media studies.

This interdisciplinary approach helps put into perspective the notion of the translatability of a text when it is transferred to a new context, and it creates a direct correspondence between *translatability* and *exportability*. The concerns over translatability and exportability help to identify the various institutions that ultimately benefit from the localization of television texts for international distribution. As the analysis of the case studies demonstrates, profits from the indigenization of texts and from micromarketing strategies that target particular national audiences represent lucrative solutions for both the exporting and the importing countries.

Put simply, what's translatable is also exportable. Such an equation plays a fundamental role at the level of production, since television executives in the United States tend to choose "translatable" scripts over ones they consider unfit for the international market. More than the concerns at the level of production, the interest in exportable products also explains the direct involvement of certain U.S. producers in the marketing strategies of their products abroad. Such strategies include, for example, the concern shown by Fox and Gracie Films regarding the choice of translators and voice-over actors to dub *The Simpsons* in foreign countries, or Fran Drescher's decision to appear on Italian television as an Italian American nanny for purposes of marketing. Further, the idea of translatability and exportability clearly concerns the foreign distributors as well, as was seen in the editorial choices employed in the translation of *The Sopranos* to avoid any possible reference to the Mafia.

Audiovisual translations also reflect certain common industrial practices that are changing with the increasing flow of international programs beyond national borders. *The Nanny*'s director of dubbing Massimo Corizza explains how in the past Italian networks would broadcast certain series months or years after their original broadcast in the United States. This scenario used to give translators and dialogue writers time to "think about the text" and make changes in a more cohesive and coherent way because they had access to the whole series in advance, not only to a few individual episodes. Until the 1990s in fact, dubbing studios used to receive entire seasons of a show, often accompanied by certain guidelines and explanations concerning cultural references made in the original text. As Corizza contends: "it is important for us who adapt the text to know the original reference in order to transfer it to the new context without making that reference absurd and incomprehensible."[1] Currently, however, there is a different kind of immediacy in the export/import of television texts, which forces translators to adapt such texts without much prior information. One of the consequences is that translators and dialogue writers ignore the overall story and the characters' development, and this situation creates many practical problems, beyond generally lowering the quality of dubbing given the time constraints. For one thing, directors of dubbing find this "narrative uncertainty" particularly difficult because they need to hire voice-over actors to dub the original actors, and the risk is to contract someone very good (and "expensive") for a character who might die in the third episode of the first season.[2]

These concerns are clearly contingent and testify to the multifaceted possibilities for indigenization that dubbing offers. Dubbing, in fact, brings in numerous opportunities for textual manipulation, an aspect that justifies the notion of dubbing as cultural ventriloquism rather than as straightforward and literal translation. It is important to point out, in fact, that the idea of dubbing as cultural ventriloquism entails certain relations of power. Dubbing, especially when it is well done, even if more inexpensive in comparison with any kind of actual production, is still more expensive than subtitling. Thus, in order for one country to have its voice heard in translation, that country needs to be wealthy enough to be able to afford dubbing; otherwise those national networks may have to opt for subtitling, which offers less effective possibilities for indigenization.

The research in this book was based on Italy, a Western country and member state of the European Union that has both a long tradition of dubbing and the resources to translate and reformat imported foreign programs. Further and future analysis should focus on less wealthy nations and developing countries in order to consider whether similar negotiations between the global and the local can be developed through dubbing and translation, or whether there are other more effective strategies for indigenization in non-Western nations. In other words, if dubbing through the manipulation of texts allows one country to "represent" itself in the processes of translation and indigenization of foreign products, what needs to be addressed is what happens to those countries that do not have the resources for dubbing and are forced to use less "intrusive" (which also means less powerful) methods of translation.

Notes

Introduction

1. Stangor and Schaller, "Stereotypes as Individual and Collective Representations," 11.
2. Maas and Arcuri, "Language and Stereotyping," 193.
3. Ibid., 194.
4. Ascheid, "Speaking Tongues," 40.
5. Italian dialogue writer Serafino Murri contends, "It is not so much about learning to translate 'something,' but to gain the skills to understand the 'linguistic game,' as Wittgenstein would call it, to perceive language as 'use'—a sort of skill one cannot gain without hitting one's head a hundred times against what is untranslatable" ("Lo scrittore che non c'è," 81).
6. Shohat and Stam, "Cinema After Babel," 42.
7. Lotman, *Universe of the Mind,* 127.
8. This idea is shaped by Benedict Anderson's idea of imagined communities together with Homi Bhabha's conception of national (and nationalistic) allegories and modes of narration. Anderson's influential work argues that the nation is "an imagined political community," and thus such national "communities are to be distinguished by the style in which they are imagined." In other words, Anderson argues that by envisioning groups of people sharing political, religious, and historical myths and experiences, the idea of the nation is created along with a sense of belonging to it. Discussing modern western European countries, Anderson claims that "print-capitalism" has provided significant impulses for such processes of imagining national communities, allowing a heightened sense of belonging to specific nations. See Anderson, *Imagined Communities,* 6.

Given the importance and the ubiquitous nature of visual information in contemporary late-capitalist societies, my project shifts from an analysis of late nineteenth- and early twentieth-century *print* media (as discussed by Anderson) to a study of late twentieth- and early twenty-first-century *visual* media. Thus, my approach substitutes television for print-capitalism as recounting narratives of the nation while reinforcing the formation of imagined and represented national communities on the basis of stereotypical myths of the nation.

Imagining and *narrating*—and consequently *representing*—the nation according to established conventions are fundamental aspects of television. TV networks, in fact, often create representations and cultural tales on the basis of accepted stereotypes and ideas about their national audiences, and employ narrative strategies and modes of narration with which such audiences are familiar. In this respect, Homi Bhabha's theoretical formulation about *"narrating* the nation" explains television texts as constructing and recounting culturally specific stories of the homeland. Bhabha claims, "The ambivalent antagonist perspective of nation as narration will establish the cultural boundaries of the nation so that they may be acknowledged as 'containing' thresholds of meaning that must be crossed, erased, and translated in the process of cultural production" ("Introduction," 4).

My analysis adopts a specific perspective within this framework: through the construction of national narratives (and the consequent production of culture), certain "imagined televisual representations" are created, with the goal of marketing to niche—and specific national—audiences. Once television programs are exported abroad, however, the process of imagining, narrating, and representing the nation needs to start over in order to produce new national cultures for new national audiences. Bhabha claims, in fact, that for any constructed metaphor of a nation, "there must also be a tribe of interpreters of such metaphors—the translators of the dissemination of texts and discourses across cultures" ("DissemiNation," 293). In Bhabha's view, then, any kind of "dissemination of texts" must undergo a process of translation and indigenization for such texts to resonate and produce new cultural narratives within their new context. Seen from this perspective, the import and export of media programs across different cultures and nations is nothing but a particular version of dissemination of texts that need to be indigenized for new national audiences. Translators, therefore, make possible and facilitate the production of new cultures according to established metaphors of the new nation in which they operate—metaphors that should have a correspondence with the original narratives disseminated.

Chapter 1

1. This introductory discussion on Italian television has been re-elaborated from an earlier piece I wrote with Michela Ardizzoni, titled "Introduction: Italian Media Between the Local and the Global." In *Beyond Monopoly: Contemporary Italian Media and Globalization,* ed. Michela Ardizzoni and Chiara Ferrari (Lanham, Md.: Lexington Books, 2009), xi–xix.

2. Bechelloni, "Italy."

3. In the late 1970s and early 1980s, European television, traditionally regulated by centralized federal governments, opened to private ownership. This deregulatory process caused the proliferation of channels as new networks were added, providing alternatives to the various national broadcasting systems. Ever since deregulation, television in Europe has been characterized by a significant increase in the number of hours of programming, which necessitated a corresponding increase in content. Channels that used to air only at specific times of

the day suddenly needed to cover twenty-four-hour schedules, given the necessity of nighttime programming caused by the increasing competition among networks. Soon national production was unable to fill the demand of the broadcasters to cover the new schedule of programming. Such a shift in the European broadcasting system created the need for more imported programs to differentiate the selection of products offered. Network competition, in fact, was based not only on increased hours of programming, but also on the ability to ensure new and interesting products less related to local and regional environments, and to offer broader and more diverse points of view to the audience.

The deregulation of the 1970s–1980s and the subsequent turn toward increased importation mark the beginning of European commercial television. This shift stood in stark contrast to the older and more nationally based concept of public television broadcasting. It also marks a much stronger embrace of the American model, since U.S. television began as a commercial enterprise, as opposed to the European "educational" model.

4. Known officially as Commissione Parlamentare per l'Indirizzo Generale e la Vigilanza dei Servizi Radiotelevisivi (Parliamentary Commission for the General Address and Supervision of [Public] Broadcast Services), the 1975 authority committee was created to ensure more pluralism in the Italian public TV system. Generally speaking, while the Italian government includes only those political parties that have received the majority of votes and (currently) hold power, the Parliament comprises a multitude of parties and senators that do not necessarily and exclusively reflect the leading political ideas represented by the prime minister (in charge of the government, but not of the Parliament). The parliamentary commission includes forty members, who elect a president, a vice president, and two secretaries among themselves. The chosen president is usually part of and politically in line with one of the opposition parties (information available from the Italian Parliament official Web site: http://www.parlamento.it/bicamerali/43775/43777/48818/48821/paginabicamerali.htm).

5. Information available from the Mediaset Corporate Group Web site: http://www.mediaset.it/corporate/chisiamo/storia_en.shtml.

6. Barron, "Berlusconi."

7. Berlusconi's "dictatorial approach" toward the media in the years of his mandate as prime minister caused many respected journalists and entertainers at RAI to be fired in a matter of days. In the infamous speech from Sofia in 2002, Berlusconi accused journalists Enzo Biagi, Michele Santoro, and Daniele Luttazzi of making a "criminal use of TV" when questioning his rise to politics; they lost their jobs shortly thereafter and were able to return to the air only after Romano Prodi's victory in the 2006 elections for prime minister.

8. Bechelloni, "Televisione e nazionalizzazione degli italiani," 438.

9. Morley and Robins, *Spaces of Identity*, 44.

10. Although originally not American, formats such as *Deal Or No Deal* and *Big Brother* have become the symbols of contemporary global television since the Endemol Group has been producing formulas that have been able to travel worldwide, including to the United States, creating an international environment for reformatting.

11. Ardizzoni, "Taming the Global on Italian Television."

12. Nobili interview with author.

13. Forgacs, "Mass Media and the Question of a National Community in Italy," 143.

14. Grasso, *Storia della televisione italiana.*

15. Ibid., xiii.

16. Forgacs, "Mass Media and the Question of a National Community in Italy," 149–50.

17. Forgacs, *Italian Culture in the Industrial Era,* 28.

18. Moss, "Language and Italian National Identity," 109.

19. Moran, *Copycat TV,* 175–176.

20. Centro Studi e Richerche Idos, *Immigrazione dossier statistico, 2008: XVIII rapporto sull'immigrazione* (Rome: Caritas/Migrantes, 2008), 1.

21. Grasso, *Storia della televisione italiana,* 769.

22. John Dickie, "Imagined Italies." In *Italian Cultural Studies: An Introduction,* ed. David Forgacs and Robert Lumley (New York: Oxford University Press, 1996), 27–28.

23. Corizza interview with author.

24. In other words, the fact that Italians now know what pancakes are does not mean that Italians have changed their eating habits accordingly. In most Italian cities, in fact, the regular breakfast is still based on the consumption of cappuccino and *brioche,* as opposed to pancakes. Vice versa, drinking Coke and eating hamburgers in Italy are not direct symptoms of a progressive move toward individualism, entrepreneurship, and capitalism—values usually and stereotypically associated with the United States.

25. Moran, *Copycat TV,* 171–172.

26. As will be further explored in Chapter 2 and Chapter 5, Buonanno discusses the paradigm of indigenization in terms of both domestication and foreignization, arguing that "making familiar an extra-ordinary phenomenon or, on the contrary, making strange a familiar phenomenon, offer excellent cognitive and narrative approaches." Buonanno, *Indigeni si diventa,* xii, 5.

27. As analyzed more in depth in Chapter 5, Italian television networks tend to prefer for airing in their prime time nationally produced miniseries that develop within four to six episodes, often based on the lives of famous historical or religious figures, narrated in a highly melodramatic fashion, and generally conceived for family viewing. This type of "format"—the *sceneggiato*—is considered more profitable for prime time and could be considered the quintessential mark of Italian television productions.

28. Harrington and Bielby clarify the idea of layers of localization by discussing some of the strategies applied by television executives when both importing and exporting television programs: "Those involved on the production and distribution side of international syndication as well as buyers in receiving countries recognize that many aspects of television programming, like any other cultural product, do not necessarily translate across borders and must be adapted to do so. As a result, some genres of programs are selectively marketed to specific regions, producers and syndicators often allow buyers to control editing and other modifications for their markets, and producers sometimes avoid certain themes and language in anticipation of the decisions of gatekeepers in foreign markets." Harrington and Bielby, "Markets and Meanings," 222.

29. One of the most significant studies on European fiction can be found in the annual reports carried out by *Eurofiction*, a Pan-European institution that monitors television content in the member states of the EU.

30. Robertson, "Glocalization," 28.

Chapter 2

The quotes in the epigraph are translated from an online forum on dubbing in which users animatedly discuss the pros and cons of the practices of audio-visual translation. The original quotes in Italian are available from: http://www.letterealdirettore.it/forum/showthread.php?s=&threadid=2704.

1. The concern about the number of foreign programs imported and broadcast on European television, and other concerns about safeguarding European networks from the homogenizing threat of globalization, have been the focus of several media and cultural policies aimed at supporting the EU media sector. A significant step toward diversity and a conscious effort to counteract the supremacy of American television products on European networks was made in 1989 with the introduction of the Television Without Frontiers (TVWF) Directive, "the cornerstone of the European Union's audiovisual policy." With TVWF, the European Parliament aims to "ensure that all the residents in the EU have access to all EU broadcasts which have become possible with satellite and cable technology." TVWF, in fact, rests on two fundamental principles: "the free movement of European television programs within the internal market and the requirement for TV channels to reserve, whenever possible, more than half of their transmission time for European works (broadcasting quotas)." In addition to promoting European media flows and access, "the TVWF Directive also safeguards certain important public interest objectives, such as cultural diversity, the protection of minors, and the right of reply." The TVWF Directive has been and still is an invaluable tool to protect European networks against the hegemonic flood of U.S. media products. The directive has been revised in 1997, in 2003, and is currently under further examination, and its focus has been increasingly that of promoting cultural diversity within EU member states. In order to do so, great importance is still given to the single nations' broadcasting systems and regulations, so that specific national expressions can be maintained within the broader Pan-European environment. Information about the current regulations of the Television Without Frontiers Directive are available from: http://ec.europa.eu./avpolicy/reg/tvwf/index_en.htm.

2. König, "Cultural Diversity and Language Policy," 401.

3. The document, a draft report compiled by the European Parliament Committee on Culture and Education for the mandate 2004–2009, is available from: http://www.europarl.eu.int/meetdocs/2004_2009/documents/am/577/577051/577051en.pdf. The above quotes refer respectively to Amendment 42, article 1, paragraph 2, proposed by Bernat Joan i Marí, and Amendment 41, proposed by Helga Trüpel.

4. Amendments 57 and 61.

5. Information available from *ASINC*, an Italian online journal devoted to dubbing criticism: http://www.asinc.it/as_01_01.html; and from the Euro-

pean Commission for the Media's Web site: http://ec.europa.eu/information _society/media/overview/evaluation/studies/index_en.htm.

6. Di Fortunato and Paolinelli, *Tradurre per il doppiaggio,* 112.

7. Kilborn, "Speak My Language," 642.

8. Two notable exceptions are Natasa Durovicova's article "Translating America: The Hollywood Multilinguals, 1929–1933" and Abé Marlus Nornes's *Cinema Babel: Translating Global Cinema.*

9. As I will further analyze below, I base my analysis of dubbing as "cultural ventriloquism," relying mainly on Antje Ascheid's discussion of audiovisual translation in her article "Speaking Tongues: Voice Dubbing in the Cinema as Cultural Ventriloquism" and Richard Kilborn's "Speak My Language: Current Attitudes to Television Subtitling and Dubbing." For a historical and cultural discussion of ventriloquism not directly related to audiovisual translation, a good source is Steven Connor's *Dumbstruck: A Cultural History of Ventriloquism.*

10. Dibbets, "Introduction of Sound," 213.

11. Vincendeau, "Hollywood Babel," 24.

12. Dibbets, "Introduction of Sound," 213.

13. Vincendeau, "Hollywood Babel," 24.

14. According to Durovicova, "The American cinema's world markets by 1929 generated between thirty-five and forty percent of a major studio's profits" ("Translating America," 139).

15. Vindendeau, "Hollywood Babel," 33.

16. Dibbets, "Introduction of Sound," 213.

17. In particular, the Ministry of Internal Affairs (i.e., Mussolini) refused on October 22, 1930, the censorship endorsement for movies that contained dialogue in foreign languages, even if in a small amount. Mussolini claimed that Italian national cinema could not be the vehicle for foreign languages. In reality, behind the linguistic aspect of the legislation lay the effort to censor cultures that were not controlled by the regime. From Di Fortunato and Paolinelli, *Tradurre per il doppiaggio,* 6.

18. Earlier regulations preceding the Fascist regime had already highlighted the importance of the use of correct forms of Italian. In particular a censorship decree from May 31, 1914 (referring both to foreign silent movies and Italian silent productions) established that "titles, subtitles, and inter-titles had to be written in correct Italian language." From Di Fortunato and Paolinelli, *Tradurre per il doppiaggio,* 11.

19. Ibid., 12.

20. Critic Alberto Savinio denounced the language used in dubbing "without personality, asexual, bland, and colorless." Quoted in ibid., 13.

21. Ibid., 12.

22. Masterpieces of Neorealism include: *Rome, Open City* (Rossellini, 1945), *Paisan* (Rossellini, 1946), *Sciusciá* (De Sica, 1946), *The Bicycle Thief* (De Sica, 1948), and *La terra trema* (Visconti, 1948).

23. Some exceptions, however, include films belonging to the hybrid genre of *commedia all'italiana* (Italian-style comedy), which used dialects, local expressions, and accents to enhance the humor and describe characters as specific cultural personalities defined by precise stereotypes. A revealing example of this

tendency to use regional accents in the *commedia all'italiana* to refer to cultural stereotypes can be found in Mario Monicelli's *I soliti ignoti* (*Big Deal on Madonna Street*, 1958). A group of small-time crooks attempts to rob the safe of a pawnshop, but fail because of their inexperience and ineptitude. The group includes a lazy Roman boxer (who repeatedly fakes a northern Italian accent to seduce a Venetian girl), an older man from Bologna (who is constantly shown eating food), a conservative Sicilian (who locks his sister in the house until he finds a proper husband for her), and an experienced thief from Naples (who trains the group in different robbery strategies). Both the representations of the characters and the accents they use serve to make them immediately recognizable to the audience because they are based on familiar cultural, linguistic, and comic stereotypes.

24. Ibid., 438.

25. Nowell-Smith, "Italy Sotto Voce," 146.

26. "Manifesto di Amalfi" (The Amalfi manifesto) in ibid., 145.

27. "Manifesto di Amalfi," 146.

28. Nowell-Smith, "Italy Sotto Voce," 147.

29. The common and accepted idea that the purest form of Italian originally comes from the Tuscan dialect is based on the fact that Dante Alighieri developed his writing style from the "vulgar" language spoken in Florence in the thirteenth and fourteenth centuries. The use of "vulgar" Italian, the language in which he wrote the *Divina commedia,* stood in opposition to the use of Latin, which at the time was still the official language of the church and the aristocracy.

30. Di Fortunato and Paolinelli, *Tradurre per il doppiaggio,* 19.

31. The same kind of convention is usually at play in American movies and TV series that are based in foreing countries but need to portray characters speaking English so the audience can understand. In HBO's *Rome,* for example, characters speak English but are officially Roman soldiers, aristocrats, or slaves. The convention involves the casting of British actors who still speak a comprehensible language for the American audience, yet their British accent is an accepted sign of their foreignness.

32. As analyzed in Chapter 5, the representation of Italian Americans in film and television almost exclusively as mobsters creates some other problems that go beyond the possibility of an easy linguistic translation through the use of conventional and familiar accents. The fact that *The Sopranos* deals in general with the Mafia, a problematic theme to discuss on Italian media, causes actual forms of censorship imposed by the network distributing the series in Italy.

33. Nobili interview with author.

34. Accolla interview with author.

35. Patou-Patucchi interview with author.

36. Di Fortunato interview with author.

37. A complete transcript of the 2004 official national contract for *dialoghisti* is available from: http://www.aidac.it/inf_002.html and is also commented on in Di Fortunato and Paolinelli's recent volume on dubbing, *Tradurre per il doppiaggio,* 79–110.

38. Snegoff interview with author.

39. For a more in-depth discussion about the relations between media deregulation and audiovisual translation in Europe, see Kilborn, "Speak My Language."

40. Di Fortunato and Paolinelli, *Tradurre per il doppiaggio*, 100.

41. Ibid.

42. Ibid., 118.

43. Several directors of dubbing, not members of AIDAC, complain that in order to be fully effective, the national association of these practitioners should organize internal conferences and establish specific guidelines to ensure the quality of audiovisual translation. Further, they claim that often the theoretical discussions of AIDAC do not correspond to an actual improvement of the final results of dubbed products.

44. Information about the new proposal for an institution monitoring European dubbing is available from Antonio Genna's Web site, "Il mondo dei doppiatori" (http://www.antoniogenna.net/). Genna is an amateur interested in dubbing who has compiled an invaluable online resource, kept up to date with the latest information about the industry practitioners, conferences, dubbing studios, and so forth. The site is a key source for both scholars and practitioners interested in curent information about dubbing in Italy.

45. Film critic Callisto Cosulich comments on Clare Peploe's attack on dubbing in relation to the 2001 edition of the annual dubbing film festival "Voci nell'ombra": "The issue of whether or not to dub films into Italian has dragged on unresolved for the last 61 years, since *Cinema* (whose editor was none other than Vittorio Mussolini, son of the world-famous father) published an article by Michelangelo Antonioni in 1940 entitled, 'The impossible life of Clark Costa,' a legendary creature with the body of Clark Gable and the voice of Romolo Costa. That was the trigger for the two opposing camps to join in a battle that continues to the present day where the purists want to abolish a practice that the overwhelming majority of Italians consider absolutely indispensable" (Cosulich, "Dubbing Fat Hits Fire").

46. AIDAC press release in response to Clare Peploe. Available from: http://www.aidac.it/inf_001.html.

47. Groves, "Yank Pix Mine BO Gold," 72.

48. Quoted in Di Fortunato and Paolinelli, "Il doppiaggio e gli autori," 44.

49. Frau-Meigs, "Cultural Exception," 9.

50. Interview with Cavani in Di Fortunato and Paolinelli, "Il doppiaggio e gli autori," 44.

51. Frau-Meigs, "Cultural Exception," 7.

52. Edwards interview with author.

53. Benjamin, "Task of the Translator," 75.

54. Ibid., 76.

55. As further examined in Chapter 4, writer Don Payne explains how this procedure is used in *The Simpsons*. The actors first record the dialogue, and then the animation is created accordingly. Payne interview with author.

56. Kilborn, "Speak My Language," 644.

57. Ascheid, "Speaking Tongues," 33.

58. Di Fortunato and Paolinelli, *Tradurre per il doppiaggio*, 40.

59. Ascheid, "Speaking Tongues," 33.

60. Murri, "Lo scrittore che non c'è," 82.

61. Lawrence Venuti, "Introduction." In *The Translation Studies Reader,* ed. Lawrence Venuti, 2nd ed. (New York: Routledge, 2004), 20.

62. Buonanno, *Indigeni si diventa,* xiii.

63. Béhar, "Cultural Ventriloquism," 85.

64. Snegoff interview with author.

65. Michael Bakewell is cited in Kilborn, "Speak My Language," 644.

66. Quoted in Di Fortunato and Paolinelli, *Tradurre per il doppiaggio,* 21.

67. Di Carlo interview included in Federica Bologna's dissertation "*I Simpson,* la traduzione di un fenomeno culturale."

Chapter 3

1. Drescher, *Enter Whining,* 149.

2. Wilinsky, "Who Talks Like That?" 305.

3. Ibid.

4. By the end of the fifth season Fran manages to get engaged to and marry Mr. Sheffield, in Season 6 she becomes pregnant, and the series closes with Fran giving birth to twins. Such a turn in the plot officially allows Fran to move from Jewish *nanny* to Jewish *mother.*

5. Wilinsky, "Who Talks Like That?" 306.

6. Cembalest, "Big Hair, Short Skirts," 9.

7. Ibid.

8. Antler, "Epilogue," 246–247.

9. Brook, *Something Ain't Kosher Here,* 146.

10. Ardizzoni, "Redrawing the Boundaries of Italianness," 527.

11. Ibid.

12. Cembalest, "Big Hair, Short Skirts," 9.

13. Corizza interview with author.

14. Ibid.

15. Ibid.

16. Oittinen, "Teaching Translation of Fiction," 76–78.

17. Pavesi, "L'allocuzione nel doppiaggio dall'inglese al'italiano," 29.

18. Corizza interview with author.

19. Wilinsky, "Who Talks Like That?" 314.

20. Ibid., 307.

21. Ascheid, "Speaking Tongues," 33.

22. Corizza interview with author.

23. Ibid.

Chapter 4

1. El-Rashidi, "D'oh! Arabized Simpsons Not Getting Many Laughs."

2. Ibid.

3. El-Rashidi reports how some Arab viewers in Dubai, especially the younger generations, were upset at the adaptation because they had already been exposed to the original American version, and therefore knew the characters in their American setting. She explains how "many Arab blogs and Internet chat sessions have become consumed with how unfunny 'Al Shamshoon' is. 'They've ruined it! Oh yes they have, sob. . . . Why? Why, why oh why?!!!!' wrote a blogger." Even more interestingly, another blogger comments on how the network, given the significance of the changes made, should have simply produced an original Arab series set in an Arab country: "I am sure the effort [of] the people who made this show to translate it to Arabic could have made a good original show about an Egyptian family living in Egypt, dealing with religion, life and work and trying to keep a family together. That way they can proudly say Made in Egypt, instead of Made in USA Assembled in Egypt." These quotes seem to suggest that adaptations can be meaningful and successful in a new national context as long as the programs adapted are not phenomena of popular culture such as *The Simpsons*, a series that by 2005 (when it was imported to Dubai) was certainly already very well-known by its target Arab audience.

4. El-Rashidi, "D'oh! Arabized Simpsons Not Getting Many Laughs."

5. Mediaset's Ludovica Bonanome explains how translator Elena Di Carlo was chosen from three translators after a blind test proposed by Fox and Gracie Films. Once the translator was chosen, Tonino Accolla was appointed by Mediaset as dialogue writer and one of the several directors of dubbing who have rotated throughout the series. Accolla, renowned dialogue writer and voice-over actor for film dubbing, also provides Homer Simpson's Italian voice. Accolla and Bonanome interviews with author.

6. Swart, "World Gets a Kick Out of Twisted U.S. Family."

7. Ibid.

8. Beard, "Local Satire with Global Reach," 288.

9. Ibid., 289.

10. Ibid., 290.

11. Mullen, "*Simpsons* and Hanna-Barbera's Animation Legacy," 66.

12. The choice of turning to animation to renew brand image and to increase viewers was a strategy employed both by ABC and Fox, respectively, in 1966 and 1989. Fox was in the same position at the end of the 1980s as ABC was in the 1960s. In fact, "both *The Flintstones* and *The Simpsons* appeared on fledging networks that were trying to distinguish themselves through counter-programming strategies." Hilton-Morrow and McMahan, "*Flintstones* to *Futurama*," 74.

13. Mullen, "*Simpsons* and Hanna-Barbera's Animation Legacy," 82.

14. Robins, "Programming Guerillas," 39.

15. Newcomb, *TV*, 37.

16. Payne interview with author.

17. Newcomb, *TV*, 36.

18. Ott, "I'm Bart Simpson," 69.

19. Herron, "Homer Simpson's Eyes," 19.

20. Ott, "I'm Bart Simpson," 66.

21. As the *Modern Brewery Age* magazine reports: "The 'Miller Time' concept was coined in the 1970s for Miller High Life beer, but it was applied to

Miller Lite for the first time in ads that started in 1997, which featured quirky situations created by a fictional adman named Dick. That campaign that used the theme 'Anything can happen at Miller Time' was aimed at introducing the brand to younger adult drinkers but was criticized by Miller distributors as being self-absorbed and ineffective." Quote from "Miller Revives 'Miller Time' Theme for Lite," *Modern Brewery Age*, March 13, 2000. Available from: http://findarticles.com/p/articles/mi_m3469/is_11_51/ai_61622724.

22. Beard, "Local Satire with Global Reach," 275.

23. Accolla interview with author.

24. Ascheid, "Speaking Tongues," 33.

25. Armstrong, *Translation, Linguistics, Culture*, 34.

26. The French translation of *The Simpsons* offers further evidence of the cultural specificity of the show. Canadian linguist Eric Plourde explains how, given the precise references in *The Simpsons*, the show is one of the few programs that are still translated and dubbed in two different versions for France and Québec, although they share French as the official language. Plourde explains how "France and Québec have different linguistic contexts, and this has an influence on dubbing. In fact, analysis reveals that the main divergence of the practice is that Québec cartoons target a young audience, resulting in censorship or mitigation of some subversive discourse, a strategy not apparent in French dubbing" ("Dubbing of *The Simpsons*," 128).

27. Bologna, "*I Simpson*," 59.

28. Rhodes, "Flash!"

29. Buonanno, *Narrami o diva*, 163. Two major examples that come to mind are Neapolitan actor Totò, unanimously considered the "prince" of Italian comedy in film, and Eduardo De Filippo, whose theatrical plays written in the Neapolitan dialect are considered among the most genuine expressions of Italian-style comedy.

30. Bologna, "*I Simpson*," 59.

31. Vaccari, "Missed Opportunities," 217.

32. Bologna, "*I Simpson*," 64.

33. Ardizzoni, "Redrawing the Boundaries of Italianness," 526.

34. The merchandising aspect in the marketing of *The Simpsons* has clearly been a significant factor in the success of the program in the Unites States as well, but as Jason Mittell points out, the animated series has never truly been discussed in terms of U.S. children's animation. Instead, since its premiere, its creators have first and foremost described *The Simpsons* as a sitcom, which suggests that the intended audience has always been more general. See Mittell's "Cartoon Realism," 18–19.

Chapter 5

1. Venuti, "Introduction," 20.

2. Buonanno, *Indigeni si diventa*, xii–xiii.

3. Lacey, "One for the Boys?" 98.

4. Johnston, "Way North of North Jersey," 41.

5. Quoted in Lacey, "One for the Boys?" 100.

6. Hartocollis, "Enforcer Paints Picture of Gotti."

7. Newcomb, "This Is Not Al Dente," 563–564.

8. Ibid., 565.

9. Ibid.

10. Ibid., 566.

11. Lacey, "One for the Boys?" 100.

12. Safire, "Come Heavy," SM124.

13. As explained in the "official" mobspeak glossary on the HBO Web site (http://www.hbo.com/sopranos/mobspeak/), to "come heavy" means "to walk in carrying a loaded gun." Safire borrows the expression to describe the language of the series as "loaded" with cultural and social references.

14. Nobili interview with author.

15. The quotes are taken from "College," from the the first season, in which Tony answers his daughter's questions about his education while driving her to Maine to visit prospective colleges.

16. Quoted in Stanley, "Tony Soprano Goes Home," WK3.

17. As discussed in Chapter 4, out of at least ten characters in *The Simpsons* whose voices in the Italian version are translated with regional accents, only two of them speak with accents from the North, specifically from Milan and Venice.

18. Stanley, "Tony Soprano Goes Home," 3.

19. Part of this frustration was expressed in an e-mail correspondence with communication scholar Elisa Giomi. I summarize her ideas in this note. Her research focuses on the coverage of the Mafia on Italian television, in the news, in infotainment programs, and in fiction. She argues that the topic is discussed neither satisfactorily nor sufficiently on Italian television. *La Piovra*, the only series about the Mafia produced nationally, based on purely fictional characters, still managed to raise discussions and polemical debates from the first to the last season. According to Giomi the total number of programs (aired on either RAI or Mediaset) that explored the subject of the Mafia in some way was seven or eight in two years. Such programs included: a historical fiction on judge Paolo Borsellino, executed by the Mafia in 1992, broadcast by Mediaset Canale 5; Giovanni Minoli's documentary-based show (once again on Judge Borsellino) on RAI 2; a RAI docudrama, part of the series *Bluenotte* by journalist Carlo Lucarelli; and an episode of RAI 3 *Report*, the only case in which the Mafia has been discussed in an actual exploratory and analytical fashion. The arrest of Corleone boss Bernardo Provenzano in April 2006 was also discussed in infotainment programs and in less serious venues, all of which focused on the personal aspects of the boss's life, with no mention of the relations between the Mafia and politics (or how he could be on the run for forty-three years). Other examples from RAI include a TV fiction on judge Giovanni Falcone (executed by the Mafia a few months before Judge Borsellino in 1992), a couple of episodes of Michele Santoro's *Annozero*, and a "useless" episode of Bruno Vespa's *Porta a porta*, which discussed the fiction about Falcone instead of Falcone himself. Giomi contends, therefore, that the Mafia is still considered taboo on Italian television, or at least highly problematic and certainly underrepresented.

20. Bechelloni, *Televisione come cultura*, 125.

21. Ibid.

22. Milly Buonanno contends that it was precisely this unexpected domestic and international success that brought the producers of *La Piovra* to develop the series over the course of multiple seasons. What is even more interesting is that such seasons were linked together as an actual unitary corpus, something of a novelty in the traditional typology of Italian serials, which always develop and reach their closure within four to eight episodes. Buonanno, *Indigeni si diventa*, 78.

23. Grasso, *Enciclopedia della televisione*, 651.

24. Buonanno, "Un orizzonte nebuloso," 107.

25. Ibid., 108–109.

26. Buonanno, *Indigeni si diventa*, viii.

27. This is particularly true for RAI 1 (public television) and Canale 5 (private television), the channels with the highest ratings on prime time. More specific data are available from Eurofiction's annual reports. This clear preference for domestic production to fill prime-time slots is what Joseph Straubhaar has defined as "cultural proximity." In his now-classic piece "Beyond Media Imperialism: Asymmetrical Interdependence and Cultural Proximity," Straubhaar argues that "audiences make an active choice to view international or regional or national television programs, a choice that favors the latter two when they are available, based on a search for cultural relevance or preference. These audience preferences lead television industries and advertisers to produce more programming nationally and to select an increasing proportion of what is imported from within the same region, language group, and culture, when such programming is available" (39).

On the basis of the idea of the active audience, Straubhaar contends that, despite the flooding of international (American) media programs, it is undeniable that various countries and national media industries opt for those shows that are closer in to the nation's own language, culture, and geography when such countries are not able to produce their own content. In other words, national productions are often the first choice of the audience, and hence the advertisers, followed by programs from similar geo-linguistic and cultural areas. The concept of cultural and media imperialism, therefore, is much more complex than its political-economic formulation claims.

28. Buonanno, "Un orizzonte nebuloso," 114.

29. Bauder, "A&E Bets Future on 'Sopranos.'"

30. Nobili interview with the author.

31. A few censoring changes were actually made, not so much to the actual coarse language or the nudity and violence in the visuals, but to certain linguistic terms in the dialogue that linked *The Sopranos* too closely to Italian organized crime.

32. Buonanno, "Un orizzonte nebuloso," 100.

33. Buonanno, *Indigeni si diventa*, 85.

34. Bill Carter, "Last Aria of Tony Soprano," 2.

35. Nobili interview with the author.

36. "Mala" stands for *malavita,* which literally means "bad life" or "life of crime." The term refers to organized crime and therefore indirectly to Mafia as well, but it is not quite as precise or locally specific as the word "Mafia."

37. In Italy there is no such thing as Easter egg hunting, so the dialogue needed to be modified to a reference about Christmas presents.

38. Zecchinelli, "'Sopranos' Debut Attracts a Mob on Italo TV."

39. From Peter Popham, "Man Who Took on the Mafia: The Truth About Italy's Gangsters," *The Independent,* October 17, 2006. Available from: http://www.independent.co.uk/news/world/europe/man-who-took-on-the-mafia-the-truth-about-italys-gangsters-420427.html.

40. Saviano "La repubblica dei Soprano," 101.

41. Ibid.

42. Mediaset Premium press release, May 2, 2006. Available from: http://www.mediaset.it/corporate/salastampa/2006/comunicatostampa_3301_en.shtml.

43. Buonanno, "Un orizzonte nebuloso," 97.

44. Ibid., 98. Buonanno bases her discussion of paid cable and regular broadcasting in Italy on the analysis of TV fiction in 2001. In the last nine years the situation does not seem to have changed drastically, with the great majority of Italians still opting for network television programming over cable. According to *Variety,* pay TV in Italy is increasing, but the total amount of households with a DTT decoder is 5.6 million, out of 22 million TV households. Nick Vivarelli, "Cable TV, Italian Style," *Variety,* January 25, 2008.

45. For a thorough discussion about cultural discount, see Hoskins and Mirus, "Reasons for the U.S. Dominance of the International Trade in Television Programmes."

46. Bauder, "A&E Bets Future on 'Sopranos.'"

Conclusion

1. Corizza interview with author.

2. Ibid.

Selected Bibliography

Alberti, John, ed. *Leaving Springfield: The Simpsons and the Possibility of Oppositional Culture*. Detroit: Wayne State University Press, 2004.

Allen, Beverly, and Mary Russo. *Revisioning Italy: National Identity and Global Culture*. Minneapolis: University of Minnesota Press, 1997.

Altman, Rick. "Moving Lips: Cinema as Ventriloquism." *Yale French Studies* 60 (1980): 67–79.

Alvarado, Manuel. "Selling Television." In *Film Policy: International, National and Regional Perspectives*, ed. Albert Moran. London: Routledge, 1996: 62–71.

———, ed. *Trasnationalization of Television in Western Europe*. London: John Libbey, 1990.

Anderson. Benedict. *Imagined Communities*. London: Verso. 1983.

Ang, Ien. *Desperately Seeking the Audience*. London: Routledge. 1991.

———. *Watching Dallas*. London: Methuen, 1985.

Ang, Ien, and David Morley. "Mayonnaise Culture and Other European Follies." *Cultural Studies* 3 (1989): 145–165.

Antler, Joyce. "Epilogue: Jewish Women on Television." In *Talking Back: Images of Jewish Women in American Popular Culture*, ed. Joyce Antler. Hanover, N.H.: Brandeis University Press, 1998: 242–252.

Aphornsuvan, Thanet. "Communication and the Preservation of National Identity." *Media Development* 2 (1997), http://www.waccglobal.com/fr/19972-communication-and-national-identity/930-Communication-and-the-Preservation-of-National-Identity.html.

Ardizzoni, Michela. "Redrawing the Boundaries of Italianness: Televised Identities in the Age of Globalization." *Social Identities* 11 (September 2005): 509–530.

———. "Taming the Global on Italian Television." *Flow* 1 (2005), http://flowtv.org/?p=658.

Armstrong, Nigel. *Translation, Linguistics, Culture: A French-English Handbook*. Clevedon, UK: Multilingual Matters. 2005.

———. "Voicing 'The Simpsons' from English into French: A Story of Variable Success." *Cahiers* 10 (Spring–Summer 2004): 32–47.

Ascheid, Antje. "Speaking Tongues: Voice Dubbing in the Cinema as Cultural Ventriloquism." *Velvet Light Trap* 40 (Fall 1997): 32–41.

Balibar, Étienne. *We, the People of Europe? Reflections on Translational Citizenship*. Princeton, N.J.: Princeton University Press, 2004.

Barnes, Brooks. "New Accent: NBC Faces Trials Bringing *Law and Order* to France." *Wall Street Journal*, March 1, 2007.

Barron, Brian. "Berlusconi: The Billion-Dollar Question." *BBC News*, May 14, 2001. Available from: http://news.bbc.co.uk/1/hi/world/europe/1325466.stm.

Bauder, David. "A&E Bets Future on 'Sopranos.'" *Columbia Daily Tribune*, March 3, 2005. Available from: http://archive.columbiatribune.com/2005/Mar/20050303Go!013.asp.

Beard, Duncan Stuart. "Local Satire with Global Reach: Ethnic Stereotyping and Cross-Cultural Conflicts in *The Simpsons*." In *Leaving Springfield: The Simpsons and the Possibility of Oppositional Culture*, ed. John Alberti. Detroit: Wayne State University Press, 2004: 273–291.

Bechelloni, Giovanni. "Italy." Museum of Broadcasting Communications. Available from: http://www.museum.tv/archives/etv/I/htmlI/italy/italy.htm.

———. *Televisione come cultura*. Naples: Liguori, 1995.

———. "Television e nazionalizzazione degli italiani." In *La chioma della vittoria: Scritti sull'identità degli italiani dall'unità alla seconda repubblica*, ed. Sergio Bertelli. Florence: Ponte alle Grazie, 1997: 415–442.

Becchelloni, Giovanni, and Milly Buonanno. *Television Fiction and Identities: America, Europe, Nations*. Los Angeles: Ipermedium, 1997.

Béhar, Henri. "Cultural Ventriloquism." In *Subtitles: On the Foreignness of Film*, ed. Atom Egoyan and Ian Balfour. Cambridge, Mass.: MIT Press, 2004: 79–86.

Benjamin, Walter. "The Task of the Translator." In *The Translation Studies Reader*, ed. Lawrence Venuti. London: Routledge, 2000: 75–82.

Bernardi, Daniel, ed. *The Persistence of Whiteness: Race and Contemporary Hollywood Cinema*. New York: Routledge, 2008.

Bettetini, Gianfranco, and Aldo Grasso, eds. *Televisione: La provvisoria identità italiana*. Torino: Fondazione Agnelli, 1985.

Betz, Mark. "The Name Above the (Sub)Title: Internationalism, Coproduction, and Polyglot European Art Cinema." *Camera Obscura* 46 (2001): 1–45.

Bhabha, Homi. "DissemiNation: Time, Narrative, and the Margins of the Modern Nation." In *Nation and Narration*, ed. Homi Bhabha. London: Routledge, 1990: 291–322.

———. "Introduction: Narrating the Nation." In *Nation and Narration*, ed. Homi Bhabha. New York: Routledge, 1990: 1–7.

Bicket, Douglas. "Reconsidering Geocultural Contraflow: Intercultural Information Flows Through Trends in Global Audiovisual Trade." *Global Media Journal* 4 (Spring 2005), http://lass.calumet.purdue.edu/cca/gmj/sp05/gmj-sp05-bicket.htm.

Bologna, Federica. "*I Simpson*, la traduzione di un fenomeno culturale." Dissertation, Istituto Superiore Interpreti e Traduttori, Milan, 2005–2006.

Bondanella, Peter E. *Hollywood Italians: Dagos, Palookas, Romeos, Wise Guys, and Sopranos*. New York: Continuum, 2004.

Brennan, Timothy. "The National Longing for Form." In *Nation and Narration*, ed. Homi Bhabha. London: Routledge, 1990: 44–70.

Brisset, Annie. "The Search for a Native Language: Translation and Cultural Identity." In *The Translation Studies Reader*, ed. Lawrence Venuti. London: Routledge, 2000: 337–368.

Brook, Vincent. *Something Ain't Kosher Here: The Rise of the "Jewish" Sitcom.* New Brunswick, N.J.: Rutgers University Press, 2003.

Buonanno, Milly. "Foreign Fiction: From Threat to Resource: Towards a New Critical Theory of International Television Flows." *Studies in Communication Sciences* 4 (2004): 31–47.

———. *Indigeni si diventa: Locale e globale nella serialità televisiva.* Milan: Sansoni, 1999.

———. *Narrami o diva.* Napoli: Liguori Editore, 1994.

———. "Un orizzonte nebuloso: La fiction TV italiana nel 2001." In *Eurofiction, 2002: Sesto rapporto sulla televisione in Europa*, ed. Milly Buonanno. Rome: RAI-ERI, 2002: 95–114.

Canagarajah, Suresh A., ed. *Reclaiming the Local in Language Policy and Practice.* Mahwah, N.J.: Lawrence Erlbaum Associates, 2005.

Caron, Caroline-Isabelle. "Translating Trek: Rewriting an American Icon in a Francophone Context." In *Television: The Critical View*, ed. Horace Newcomb, 7th ed. Oxford: Oxford University Press, 2006: 150–184.

Carter, Bill. "The Last Aria of Tony Soprano." *New York Times*, February 26, 2006.

Cembalest, Robin. "Big Hair, Short Skirts—and High Culture." *Forward*, February 14, 1997.

Chadha, Kalyani, and Anadam Kavoori. "Globalisation and National Media Systems: Mapping Interactions in Policies, Markets, and Formats." In *Mass Media and Society*, ed. James Curran and Michael Gurevitch, 4th ed. London: Edward Arnold, 2005: 84–103.

Chea, Sotheacheath. "The Role of Media in the Creation and Development of National Identity." *Media Development* 2 (1997), http://www.waccglobal.com/fr/19972-communication-and-national-identity/935-The-role-of-media-in-the-creation-and-development-of-national-identity.html.

Cole, Jeffrey. *The New Racism in Europe: A Sicilian Ethnography.* Cambridge: Cambridge University Press, 1997.

Connor, Steven. *Dumbstruck: A Cultural History of Ventriloquism.* Oxford: Oxford University Press, 2000.

Cosulich, Callisto. "Le polemiche sul doppiaggio." *Cinecittà News* (online dossier), October 3, 2001. Available from: http://news.cinecitta.com/dossier/articolo.asp?id=446.

Crofts Wiley, Stephen B. "Rethinking Nationality in the Context of Globalization." *Communication Theory* 14 (2004): 78–96.

Cronin, Michael. *Translation and Globalization.* London: Routledge, 2003.

———. *Translation and Identity.* London: Routledge, 2006.

Cubitt, Geoffrey, ed. *Imagining Nations.* Manchester: Manchester University Press, 1998.

Curtin, Michael. "Media Capitals: Cultural Geographies of Global TV." In *Tele-*

vision After TV, ed. Lynn Spigel and Jan Olsson. Durham, N.C.: Duke University Press, 2004: 270–302.

Curtis, Scott. "The Sound of the Early Warner Bros. Cartoons." In *Sound Theory, Sound Practice,* ed. Rick Altman. New York: Routledge, 1992: 191–203.

Cvetkovich, Ann, and Douglas Kellner, eds. *Articulating the Global and the Local: Globalization and Cultural Studies.* Boulder, CO: Westview Press, 1997.

Daly, Herman. "Globalization and Its Discontents." *Philosophy and Public Policy Quarterly* 21 (Spring–Summer 2001): 17–21.

Danan, Martine. "Dubbing as an Expression of Nationalism." *Meta* 36 (1991): 606–614.

De Bens, Els, and Hedwig de Smaele. "The Inflow of American Television Fiction on European Broadcasting Channels Revisited." *European Journal of Communication* 16 (2001): 51–76.

Delabastita, Dirk. "Translation and Mass Communication: Film and TV Translation as Evidence of Cultural Dynamics." *Babel* 35 (1989): 193–218.

———. "Translation and the Mass Media." In *Translation, History, and Culture,* ed. Susan Bassnett and André Lefevere. London: Pinter, 1990: 97–109.

De Mauro, Tullio. "Il linguaggio televisivo e la sua influenza." In *I linguaggi settoriali in italia,* ed. Gian Luigi Beccaria. Milan: Bompiani, 1973: 107–117.

———. "Lingua e dialetti." In *Stato dell'italia,* ed. Paul Ginsberg. Milan: Il Saggiatore, 1994: 61–66.

———. *L'italia delle italie.* Florence: Nuova Guaraldi Editrice, 1979.

———. *Storia linguistica dell'italia unita.* Roma: Laterza, 1991.

De Swaan, Abram. "Notes on the Emerging Global Language System: Regional, National, and Supranatural," *Media, Culture, and Society* 13 (1991): 309–324.

Dibbets, Karel. "The Introduction of Sound." In *The History of World Cinema,* ed. Geoffrey Nowell-Smith. Oxford: Oxford University Press, 1996: 211–219.

Di Fortunato, Eleonora, and Mario Paolinelli. "Il doppiaggio e gli autori: Liliana Cavani." In *Barriere linguistiche e circolazione delle opere audiovisive: La questione doppiaggio,* ed. Eleonora Di Fortunato and Mario Paolinelli. Rome: AIDAC Publications, 1996: 222–226.

———. *Tradurre per il doppiaggio.* Milan: Hoepli, 2005.

Doyle, Waddick. "Why Dallas Was Able to Conquer Italy" *Media Information Australia* 41 (February 1987): 49–52.

Drescher, Fran. *Enter Whining.* New York: Regan Books, 1997.

Dries, Josephine. *Dubbing and Subtitling: Guidelines for Production and Distribution.* Düsseldorf: European Institute for the Media, 1995.

Drummond, Phillip, Richard Patterson, and Janet Willis, eds. *National Identity and Europe: The Television Revolution.* London: BFI Publishing, 1993.

Durovicova, Natasa. "Local Ghosts: Dubbing in Early Sound Cinema." In *Il Film e i suoi multipli/Film and Its Multiples: IX Convegno Internazionale di Studi sul Cinema,* ed. Anna Antonini. Udine, Italy: Forum, 2003: 83–98.

———. "*Los Toquis,* or Urban Babel." In *Global Cities,* ed. Patrice Petro and Linda Krause. New Brunswick, N.J.: Rutgers University Press, 2003: 71-86.

————. "Translating America: The Hollywood Multilinguals, 1929–1933." In *Sound Theory, Sound Practice,* ed. Rick Altman. New York: Routledge, 1992: 138–153.

Eco, Umberto. *Apocalittici e integrati.* Milan: Bompiani, 1964.

————. *Dire quasi la stessa cosa: Esperienze di traduzione.* Milan: Bompiani, 2003.

El-Rashidi, Yasmine. "D'oh! Arabized Simpsons Not Getting Many Laughs." *Wall Street Journal,* October 14, 2005.

Extra, Guus, and Kutlay Yagmur, eds. *Urban Multilingualism in Europe: Immigrant Minority Languages at Home and School.* Clevedon, UK: Multilingual Matters, 2004.

Extra, Guus, and Ludo Verhoeven, eds. *Immigrant Languages in Europe.* Clevedon, UK: Multilingual Matters, 1993.

Featherstone, Mike, ed. *Global Culture. Nationalism, Globalization, and Modernity.* London: Sage Publications, 1990.

————. *Undoing Culture. Globalization, Postmodernism, and Identity.* London: Sage Publications, 1995.

Ferguson, Marjorie. "The Mythology About Globalization." *European Journal of Communication* 7 (1992): 69–93.

Ferrari, Chiara. "*The Nanny* in Italy: Language, Nationalism, and Cultural Identity." *Global Media Journal* 3 (Spring 2004), http://lass.calumet.purdue .edu/cca/gmj/OldSiteBackup/SubmittedDocuments/archivedpapers/ Spring2004/grad_research/refereed/ferrari.htm.

Ferrari, Chiara, and Michela Ardizzoni. "Introduction: Italian Media Between the Local and the Global." In *Beyond Monopoly: Contemporary Italian Media and Globalization,* ed. Michela Ardizzoni and Chiara Ferrari. Lanham, MD: Lexington Books, 2009: xi–xix.

Ferraro, Thomas J. *Feeling Italian: The Art of Ethnicity in America.* New York: New York University Press, 2005.

Fiske, John. "Act Globally, Think Locally." In *Planet TV: A Global Television Reader,* ed. Lisa Parks and Shanti Kumar. New York: New York University Press, 2003: 277–285.

Forgacs, David. *Italian Culture in the Industrial Era, 1880–1980.* Manchester: Manchester University Press, 1990.

————. "The Mass Media and the Question of a National Community in Italy." In *The Politics of Italian National Identity: A Multidisciplinary Perspective,* ed. Gino Bedani and Bruce Haddock. Cardiff: University of Wales Press, 2000: 142–162.

Forgacs, David, and Robert Lumley, eds. *Italian Cultural Studies: An Introduction.* Oxford: Oxford University Press, 1996.

Frau-Meigs, Divina. "'Cultural Exception,' National Policies, and Globalization: Imperatives in Democratization and Promotion of Contemporary Culture." *Quaderns del CAC* 14 (September–December 2002): 3–18.

Gallozzi, Gabriella. "L'inferno del doppiaggio nell'era del 'libero mercato.'" *L'Unità,* July 12, 2003. Available from: http://www.aidac.it/docu/rs/rs004 .u.doc.

Gilman, Sander. *The Jew's Body.* New York: Routledge, 1991.

Gomery, Douglas. "Economic Struggle and Hollywood Imperialism: Europe Converts to Sound." *Yale French Studies* 60 (1980): 80–93.

Gottlieb, Henrik. "Subtitling: A New University Discipline." In *Teaching Translation and Interpreting*, ed. Cay Dollerup and Anne Loddegaard. Philadelphia: John Benjamins Publishing, 1992: 161–170.

Grasso, Aldo. *Enciclopedia della televisione*. Milan: Garzanti, 1996.

———. *Storia della televisione italiana*. Milan: Garzanti, 2004.

Groves, Don. "Yank Pix Mine BO Gold as Euro Dubbers Get in Synch." *Variety*, August 10, 1992.

Guider, Elizabeth. "Badda-Bing Has Global Ring." *Variety*, January 13–19, 2003.

Hall, Stuart. "The Local and the Global: Globalization and Ethnicity." In *Culture, Globalization, and the World-System: Contemporary Conditions for the Representation of Identity*, ed. Anthony D. King. Minneapolis: University of Minnesota Press, 1997: 19–40.

Harcourt, Alison. "Engineering Europeanization: The Role of the European Institutions in Shaping National Media Regulation." *Journal of European Public Policy* 9 (2002): 736–755.

———. *The European Union and the Regulation of Media Markets*. New York: Palgrave, 2005.

Harrington, C. Lee, and Denise D. Bielby. "Global Television Distribution: Implications of TV 'Traveling' for Viewers, Fans, and Texts." *American Behavioral Scientist* 48 (2005): 902–920.

———. "Markets and Meanings." In *Global Culture*, ed. Diana Crane, Nobuko Kawashima, and Kenichi Kawasaki. London: Routledge, 2002: 215–232.

Hartocollis, Anemona. "Enforcer Paints Picture of Gotti as Powerful Don." *New York Times*, February 23, 2006.

Havens, Timothy. *Global Television Marketplace*. London: BFI Publishing, 2006.

Hay, James. "Invisible Cities/Visible Geographies: Toward a Cultural Geography of Italian Television in the 1990s." In *Television: The Critical View*, ed. Horace Newcomb, 6th ed. Oxford: Oxford University Press, 2000: 687–700.

Henderyckx, Françoise. "Language as the Irreducible Impediment to Transnational Television Programmes." Paper presented at the "Turbulent Europe" conference, London, 1994.

Henry, Matthew. "The Triumph of Popular Culture: Situation Comedy, Postmodernism, and *The Simpsons*." *Studies in Popular Culture* 17 (1994): 85–99.

Herron, Jerry. "Homer Simpson's Eyes and the Culture of Late Nostalgia." *Representations* 43 (Summer 1993): 1–26.

Hilton-Morrow, Wendy, and David T. McMahan. "*The Flintstones* to *Futurama*: Networks and Prime-Time Animation." In *Prime Time Animation: Television Animation and American Culture*, ed. Carol A. Stabile and Mark Harrison. London: Routledge, 2003: 74–88.

Hoppus, Mark. "American Icons: Homer Simpson: He Is Truth, He Is Everyman, He Is Doughnut: Behold the Paterfamilias of the Classic American Family." *Rolling Stone*, May 15, 2003.

Hoskins, Colin, and Rolf Mirus. "Reasons for the U.S. Dominance of the International Trade in Television Programmes." *Media, Culture, and Society* 10 (1988): 499–515.

Ito, Youichi. "Theories on the Mass Media and Ethnicity: How Do the Mass Media Affect Ethnicity and Related Problems?" In *Mass Media and Cultural Identity: Ethnic Reporting in Asia,* ed. Anura Goonasekera and Youichi Ito. London: Pluto Press, 1999: 11–30.

Jameson, Fredric, and Masao Miyoshi. *The Cultures of Globalization.* Durham, N.C.: Duke University Press, 1998.

Johnston, Dawn. "Way North of North Jersey: A Canadian Experience of *The Sopranos.*" In *This Thing of Ours: Investigating the Sopranos,* ed. David Lavery. New York: Columbia University Press, 2002: 32–41.

Kaplan, Richard L. "Blackface in Italy: Cultural Power Among Nations in the Era of Globalization." In *Global Culture: Media, Arts, Policy, and Globalization,* ed. Diane Crane, Nobuko Kawashima, and Kenichi Kawasaki. New York: Routledge, 2002: 191–211.

Kelly, John D., and Martha Kaplan. *Represented Communities: Fiji and World Decolonization.* Chicago: University of Chicago Press, 2001.

Kilborn, Richard. "Speak My Language: Current Attitudes to Television Subtitling and Dubbing." *Media, Culture, and Society* 15 (1993): 641–660.

König, Matthias. "Cultural Diversity and Language Policy." *International Social Science Journal* 51 (September 1999): 401–408.

"L'italiano? No grazie, io parlo dialetto." *Corriere della sera,* April 21, 2007. Available from: http://www.corriere.it/Primo_Piano/Cronache/2007/04 _Aprile/20/dialetti_lingua_straniera_italiani.shtml.

Lacey, Joanne. "One for the Boys? *The Sopranos* and Its Male British Audience." In *This Thing of Ours: Investigating the Sopranos,* ed. David Lavery. New York: Columbia University Press, 2002: 95–108.

Lavery, David, ed. *Reading the Sopranos.* London: I. B. Tauris, 2006.

———, ed. *This Thing of Ours: Investigating the Sopranos.* New York: Columbia University Press, 2002.

Lepschy, Anna Laura, and Arturo Tosi, eds. *Multilingualism in Italy, Past and Present.* Oxford: Legenda, 2002.

Liebes, Tamar, and Elihu Katz. *The Export of Meaning: Cross-Cultural Readings of Dallas.* Oxford: Polity Press, 1993.

Loshitzky, Yosefa. "Travelling Culture/Travelling Television." *Screen* 37 (Winter 1996): 323–335.

Lotman, Yuri M. *Universe of the Mind: A Semiotic Theory of Culture.* Translated by Ann Shukman. London: I. B. Tauris, 1990.

Maas, Ann, and Luciano Arcuri. "Language and Stereotyping." In *Stereotypes and Stereotyping,* ed. Neil Macrae, Charles Stangor, and Miles Hewstone. New York: Guilford Press, 1996: 193–226.

Magder, Ted. "Transnational Media, International Trade, and the Idea of Cultural Diversity." *Continuum: Journal of Media and Cultural Studies* 18 (2004): 380–397.

Marchisio, Pierluca, and Guido Michelone. *I Simpson: L'allucinazione di una sit-com.* Roma: Castelvecchi, 1999.

Marziali, Manuela. *I Simpson e la tradizione culturale americana*. Siena: Prospettiva Editrice, 2003.

McFadyen, Stuart, Colin Hoskins, and Adam Finn. "The Effect of Cultural Differences on the International Co-production of Television Programs and Feature Films." *Canadian Journal of Communication* 23 (1998), http://www.cjc-online.ca/index.php/journal/article/viewArticle/1063/969.

McGarty, Craig. "Stereotype Formation as Category Formation." In *Stereotypes as Explanations,* ed. Craig McGarty, Vincent Y. Yzerbyt, and Russell Spears. Cambridge: Cambridge University Press, 2002: 16–37.

McGarty, Craig, Vincent Y. Yzerbyt, and Russell Spears. "Social, Cultural, and Cognitive Factors in Stereotype Formation." In *Stereotypes as Explanations,* ed. Craig McGarty, Vincent Y. Yzerbyt, and Russell Spears. Cambridge: Cambridge University Press, 2002: 1–15.

Menduni, Enrico. *I linguaggi della radio e della televisione*. Bari: Editori Laterza, 2006.

Miller, Toby, and George Yúdice, eds. *Cultural Policy*. Thousand Oaks, CA: Sage, 2002.

Miller, Toby, and Justin Lewis, eds. *Critical Cultural Policy Studies: A Reader.* Malden, MA: Blackwell, 2003.

Miller, Toby, Nitin Govil, John McMurria, Ting Wang, and Richard Maxwell, eds. *Global Hollywood*. London: British Film Institute, 2001.

Mittel, Jason. "Cartoon Realism: Genre Mixing and the Cultural Life of *The Simpsons.*" *Velvet Light Trap* 47 (Spring 2001): 15–28.

Monteleone, Franco, ed. *Cult Series*. 2 vols. Rome: Audino Editore, 2005.

———. *Storia della radio e della television in italia*. Venice: Marsilio, 1995.

Moran, Albert. *Copycat TV. Globalisation, Program Formats, and Cultural Identity*. Luton, UK: University of Luton Press, 1998.

———, ed. *Film Policy: International, National, and Regional Perspectives*. London: Routledge, 1996.

Moran, Albert, with Justin Malbon. *Understanding the Global TV Format*. Bristol, UK: Intellect Books, 2006.

Morley, David. "Electronic Communications and Domestic Rituals: Cultural Consumption and the Production of European Cultural Identities." In *Media Cultures,* ed. Michael Skovmand and Kim Christian Schrøder. London: Routledge, 1992: 48–69.

———. *Home Territories: Media, Mobility, and Identity*. London: Routledge, 2000.

———. "Where the Global Meets the Local: Notes from the Sitting Room." In *Planet TV: A Global Television Reader,* ed. L. Parks and S. Kumar. New York: New York University Press, 2003: 286–302.

Morley, David, and Kevin Robins. *Spaces of Identity: Global Media, Electronic Landscapes, and Cultural Boundaries*. London: Routledge, 1995.

Morris, Nancy. "The Myth of Unadulterated Media Meets the Threat of Imported Media." *Media, Culture, and Society* 24 (2002): 278–289.

Morris Nancy, and Silvio Waisbord, eds. *Media and Globalization: Why the State Matters*. Lanham, MD: Rowman and Littlefield, 2001.

Moss, Howard. "Language and Italian National Identity." In *The Politics of Ital-*

ian National Identity: A Multidisciplinary Perspective, ed. Gino Bedani and Bruce Haddock. Cardiff: University of Wales Press, 2000: 98–123.

Mullen, Megan. *"The Simpsons* and Hanna-Barbera's Animation Legacy." In *Leaving Springfield: The Simpsons and the Possibility of Oppositional Culture,* ed. John Alberti. Detroit: Wayne State University Press, 2004: 63–84.

Murri, Serafino. "Lo scrittore che non c'è." In *Barriere linguistiche e circolazione delle opere audiovisive: La questione doppiaggio,* ed. Eleonora Di Fortunato and Mario Paolinelli. Rome: AIDAC Publications, 1996: 80–85.

Negus, Keith, and Patria Román-Velázquez. "Globalization and Cultural Identities." In *Mass Media and Society,* ed. James Curran and Michael Gurevitch, 3rd ed. London: Arnold, 2000: 329–345.

Newcomb, Horace. "'This Is Not Al Dente': *The Sopranos* and the New Meaning of 'Television.'" In *Television the Critical View,* ed. Horace Newcomb, 7th ed. Oxford: Oxford University Press, 2006: 561–578.

———. *TV: The Most Popular Art.* Garden City, N.Y.: Anchor Press, 1974.

Noam, Eli. *Television in Europe.* Oxford: Oxford University Press, 1992.

Nornes, Abé Markus. *Cinema Babel: Translating Global Cinema.* Minneapolis: University of Minnesota Press, 2007.

Nowell-Smith, Geoffrey. "Italy Sotto Voce." *Sight and Sound* 37 (Summer 1968): 145–147.

Nowell-Smith, Geoffrey, and Steven Ricci, eds. *Hollywood and Europe: Economics, Culture, National Identity, 1945–95.* London: BFI Publishing, 1998.

Ohmann, Richard, ed. *Making and Selling Culture.* Hanover, N.H.: University Press of New England, 1996.

Oittinen, Riitta. "Teaching Translation of Fiction: A Dialogic Point of View." In *Teaching Translation and Interpreting,* ed. Cay Dollerup and Anne Loddegaard. Philadelphia: John Benjamins Publishing, 1992: 75–80.

Ott, Brian. "'I'm Bart Simpson, Who the Hell Are You?': A Study in Postmodern Identity (Re)Construction." *Journal of Popular Culture* 37 (August 2003): 56–81.

Padovani, Cinzia. *A Fatal Attraction: Public Television and Politics in Italy.* Lanham, MD: Rowman and Littlefield, 2005.

Paolinelli, Mario. *La professionalità negata.* Rome: AIDAC Publications, 1994.

Parks, Lisa, and Shanti Kumar, eds. *Planet TV: A Global Television Reader.* New York: New York University Press, 2003.

Pavesi, Maria. "L'allocuzione nel doppiaggio dall'inglese al'italiano." In *Il Doppiaggio: Trasposizioni Linguistiche e Culturali,* ed. Raffaella Baccolini, Rosa Maria Bollettieri Bosinelli, and Laura Gavioli. Bologna: CLUEB, 1994: 27–31.

Pieracci, Alessandra. "Datemi un medico nero in TV." *La Stampa,* September 19, 2006.

Plourde, Eric. "The Dubbing of *The Simpsons:* Cultural Appropriation, Discursive Manipulation, and Divergences." *Texas Linguistic Forum* 44 (2000): 114–131.

Polan, Dana. "Globalism's Localisms." In *Global/Local: Cultural Production and the Translational Imaginary,* ed. Rob Wilson and Wimal Dissanayake. Durham, N.C.: Duke University Press, 1996: 255–283.

————. *The Sopranos.* Durham, N.C.: Duke University Press, 2009.

Pulgram, Ernst. *The Tongues of Italy.* Cambridge, MA: Harvard University Press, 1958.

Rhodes, Joe. "Flash! 24 Simpsons Stars Reveal Themselves." *TV Guide,* October 21, 2000. Available from: http://www.snpp.com/other/articles/flash.html.

Robertson, Ronald. "Glocalization: Time-Space and Homogeneity-Heterogeneity." In *Global Modernities,* ed. Mike Featherson, Scott Lasch, and Roland Robertson. London: Sage, 1995: 25–44.

Robins, J. Max. "Programming Guerillas: Rebels With a 'Cos'?" *Variety,* June 6, 1990.

Robins, Kevin. "Reimagined Communities? European Image Spaces, Beyond Fordism." *Cultural Studies* 3 (1989): 145–165.

Safire, William. "Come Heavy: The Base Tenor of Sopranos Talk." *New York Times,* February 27, 2000.

Saviano, Roberto. "La repubblica dei Soprano." *L'Espresso,* January 3, 2008.

"SCADPlus: Pursuit of Televisual Broadcasting." Activities of the European Union summaries of legislation. Available from: http://europa.eu/legislation_summaries/audiovisual_and_media/l24101_en.htm.

Schiller, Herbert. *Culture, Inc.: The Corporate Takeover of Public Expression.* New York: Oxford University Press, 1989.

————. "Not Yet the Post-imperialist Era." *Critical Studies in Mass Communication* 8 (1991): 13–28.

Schulte, Rainer, and John Biguenet, eds. *Theories of Translation: An Anthology of Essays from Dryden to Derrida.* Chicago: University of Chicago Press, 1992.

Segrave, Kerry. *American Television Abroad: Hollywood's Attempt to Dominate World Television.* Jefferson, N.C.: McFarland, 1998.

Shohat, Ella, and Robert Stam. "The Cinema After Babel: Language, Difference, Power." *Screen* 26 (1985): 35–58.

Sinclair, John, Elizabeth Jacka, and Stuart Cunningham. *New Patterns in Global Television: Peripheral Vision.* Oxford: Oxford University Press, 1996.

Smith, Anthony. *Myths and Memories of the Nation.* Oxford: Oxford University Press, 1999.

Spivak, Gayatri Chakravorty. "The Politics of Translation." In *The Translation Studies Reader,* ed. Lawrence Venuti, 2nd ed. New York: Routledge, 2004: 369–388.

Stangor, Charles, and Mark Schaller. "Stereotypes as Individual and Collective Representations." In *Stereotypes and Stereotyping,* ed. Neil Macrae, Charles Stangor, and Miles Hewstone. New York: Guilford Press, 1996: 3–37.

Stanley, Alessandra. "Tony Soprano Goes Home." *New York Times,* June 17, 2001.

Steiner, George. *After Babel: Aspects of Language and Translation.* 2nd ed. Oxford: Oxford University Press, 1992.

Straubhaar, Joseph. "Beyond Media Imperialism: Asymmetrical Interdependence and Cultural Proximity." *Critical Studies in Mass Communication* 8 (1991): 39–59.

————. "Distinguishing the Global, Regional, and National Levels of World Television." In *Media in Global Context: A Reader,* ed. Annabelle Sreberny-

Mohammadi, Dwayne Winseck, Jim McKenna, and Oliver Boyd-Barrett. London: Arnold, 1997: 284–298.

———. *Theorizing World Television*. Thousand Oaks, CA: Sage, 2007.

Swart, Sharon. "World Gets a Kick Out of Twisted U.S. Family." *Variety,* April 23, 1998. Available from: http://www.snpp.com/other/articles/world kick.html.

Taylor, Christopher. *Language to Language: A Practical and Theoretical Guide for Italian/English Translators*. Cambridge: Cambridge University Press, 1998.

Thomson, Patricia. "Italian Renaissance: Accenting the Regional." *Village Voice,* May 21–27, 2003.

Tomlinson, John. "A Phenomenology of Globalization? Giddens on Global Modernity." *European Journal of Communication* 9 (1994): 149–172.

———. *Cultural Imperialism*. London: Pinter, 1991.

Tosi, Arturo. *Crossing Barriers and Bridging Cultures: The Challenges of Multilingual Translation for the European Union*. Clevedon, UK: Multilingual Matters, 2003.

———. *Language and Society in a Changing Italy*. Clevedon, UK: Multilingual Matters, 2001.

Vaccari, Cristian. "Missed Opportunities: The Debate on Immigrants' Voting Rights in Italian Newspapers and Television." In *Beyond Monopoly: Contemporary Italian Media and Globalization,* ed. Michela Ardizzoni and Chiara Ferrari. Lanham, MD: Lexington Books, 2009: 203–224.

Vincendeau, Ginette. "Hollywood Babel." *Screen* 29 (Spring 1998): 24–39.

Waisbord, Silvio. "McTV: Understanding the Global Popularity of Television Formats." *Television and New Media* 5 (2004): 359–383.

Waters, Jay. "Why 'Prime Time' Is a TV Sales Pitch." *B&T,* November 1, 2002.

Whitman-Linsen, Candace. *Through the Dubbing Glass: The Synchronization of American Motion Pictures into German, French, and Spanish*. New York: Peter Lang, 1992.

Wilinsky, Barbara. "'Who Talks Like That?' Foregrounding Stereotypes on *The Nanny*." In *Mediated Women: Representation in Popular Culture,* ed. Marian Meyers. Cresskill, N.J.: Hampton Press, 1996: 305–320.

Wilson, Rob, and Wimal Dissanayake, eds. *Global/Local: Cultural Production and the Translational Imaginary*. Durham, N.C.: Duke University Press, 1996.

Zabalbeascoa, Patrick. "Translating Jokes for Dubbed Television Situation Comedies." *The Translator* 2 (1996): 235–258.

Zecchinelli, Cecilia. "'Sopranos' Debut Attracts a Mob on Italo TV." *Variety,* May 28–June 3, 2001.

Zurawik, David. *The Jews of Prime Time*. Hanover, N.H.: Brandeis University Press, 2003.

Interviews

Accolla, Tonino. Interview with author. Rome, Italy: July 12, 2005.

Bonanome, Ludovica. Interview with author. Rieti, Italy: September 17, 2005.

Corizza, Massimo. Interview with author. Rome, Italy: September 20, 2005.
Di Fortunato, Eleonora. Interview with author. Rome, Italy: September 17, 2005.
Edwards, Marion. Interview with author. Los Angeles: March 22, 2006.
Nobili, Daniela. Interview with author. Rome, Italy: September 19, 2005.
Paolinelli, Mario. Interview with author. Rome, Italy: September 17, 2005.
Patou-Patucchi, Sergio. Interview with author. Rome, Italy: September 17, 2005.
Payne, Don. Interview with author. Los Angeles: April 23, 2007.
Snegoff, Gregory. Interview with author. Los Angeles: October 26, 2004.

Index